92 WOODSON 2010

Woodson, Nancy Leake.
Hurdles /

SWTR   03/16/11   1

SOUTHWEST REGIONAL

HURDLES

I find myself viewing the many beautiful colors in the rainbow as if I were looking through the sheer lens of a kaleidoscope. The many shades of color remind me of the "Hurdles" in my life.

Nancy Leake Woodson

authorHOUSE®

AuthorHouse™
1663 Liberty Drive
Bloomington, IN 47403
www.authorhouse.com
Phone: 1-800-839-8640

This book represents a true story. Some names have been changed. Where names have been changed, any resemblance to actual persons is purely coincidental. All emails are true in fact and detail. The names other than family members have been changed to provide the reader with accurate background and credible timeline.

First published by AuthorHouse 10/13/2010

ISBN: 978-1-4490-4883-9 (e)
ISBN: 978-1-4490-4881-5 (sc)
ISBN: 978-1-4490-4882-2 (hc)

Library of Congress Control Number: 2010911302

Printed in the United States of America

This book is printed on acid-free paper.

Because of the dynamic nature of the Internet, any Web addresses or links contained in this book may have changed since publication and may no longer be valid. The views expressed in this work are solely those of the author and do not necessarily reflect the views of the publisher, and the publisher hereby disclaims any responsibility for them.

Acknowledgements

Doug - My true Oz. You have loved and supported me through good times and bad. Your wisdom is real and your heart is true. You are a good man. Your ability to coach multiple teams without having your own child on the squad reminds me of why I fell in love with you because of your heart. The difference you have made in these boy's lives will be life-changing; as you have become a mentor/coach they will always remember. At the end of the day, a man's reputation is all he really has and you my friend will depart from this world with a solid standing. You have encouraged me to complete my goal and for that I will be forever grateful. Thank you and I love you.

Bailey, Jay and Lawrence - The three of you have validated my life. It is because of your existence, I have grown into the woman I am today. Your life reminds me daily of God's true love and grace, and I am proud to call each one of you my child. This book represents your true character and how I have embraced your wisdom and loving heart. Thank you for showing and teaching me your life lessons ...... the three of you are my true north!

Mother and Dad - As the road has been difficult, your love has led me into a more accepting mindset. You have taught me to listen to God's direction and never question his timing. I have learned through you both of life trials and tribulations and that we all must remain true to our self and listen to our inner voice. Although our time on earth is limited, we are on God's plan and his timing is perfect. We must always trust, love and forgive!

Kristen Crane and Susanne Cato – Thank you for all your love and support. I love you both. You both have been wonderful little sisters, but at the same time encouraged me as big sisters do.

Anne Marie Rozelle Bratton – Your artistic ability takes my breath away combined with your generosity. I love your talented cover for this book, but what I truly admire about you is how you share your gifts with everyone. You embraced Lawrence Woodson and for that I will be forever grateful. Thank you from the bottom of my heart.

Allison and Bryan Wagner – You both inspire me more than you will ever know. The four of us started this "marriage" thing together and through our friendship we will continue "One Day at a Time." After all "Our Friends are our Family."

Arma Guzman – A woman of whom I admire. Your determination as a cancer survivor while caring for your family and working full time still amazes me to this day. Thank you for taking me under your wing.

Beth Podesta Blumenfeld and Patte Hart Grant – We have come a long way from 1st grade. "Old Friends are the Best."

Bobby Pidgeon – We have come a long way from the high school days to our sons rooming together in college. Thank you for all your support with this project.

Bonnie Epstein – You are the smartest friend I have with the biggest heart. Thank you for loving my family as your own.

Big Lawrence and John Cowart - You both have been true friends as well as providing the "Woody Douglas Suite." Thank you for your generous and loving spirit.

Cary Zepernick – I love you like my own daughter. Thank you for sharing your mother/my sister with me. Your mother would be so proud of you. We will always have our green socks!

Carrie and Patrick Woodson – You two are the best! Thank you for loving and supporting our family.

Chad Woodson – I love being your big sister!

Chris Uchacz – Thank you for advising me and for being my friend. You always believed in me and I will always be grateful for your many words of encouragement and support.

Christina Johnson, Carroll Marion Kobs, Mary Carter Starkey and Carolyn Roberts – My favorite TVS girls! Thank you for welcoming me into your hometown with open arms. Love you all!

Ann Clinkscales, Kelly Nichols, Caren Parten, Adrienne Relyea, Anne Self and Lynne Thompson – Thank you all for the wisdom you each have shared with me as well as your loving heart. You girls rock!

Cindy Beard Hayes – You have been an outstanding role model, mentor and boss. Thank you for instilling in me an incredible work ethic.

Dana Cate Kelly – We have come a long way from the Delta days from Oxford, Mississippi to Fort Worth, Texas. I am so happy you followed your heart to Cowtown.

Debi Iba – It is hard to put into words just how much I admire you and your strength as an educated woman. You advised me during the darkest time in my life, but your positive encouragement always lifted me up. I will be forever grateful to you for your friendship and academic guidance.

Edmund Schenecker – Thank you for encouraging me Yoga Man! You are the best.

John and Bill Zepernick – You both will always be known as my sister Terry's twin boys. You both have turned out to be outstanding individuals and I am so proud of you both.

Kathleen and Randall Stepp – You made Lawrence feel so loved during her release from school. Your encouragement and stand for the "right" thing did not pan out as we had hoped for, but it meant the world to our entire family to have you both by our side. Thank you.

Keli Simon – Thank you for your loving heart and support.

Kip Patterson – Your support during the last few years has been a real treat. Our friendship has brought me laughter – thanks - I needed that!

Hal Brown – You hired me from the trenches of motherhood as your Promotional Director for our City's Magazine and advanced me to an account executive within twelve months. You believed in me and I will always be grateful.

Lee Gattas Proctor – You are my favorite person ever but please don't tell anyone. I love you.

Mr. Woodson – You are my favorite artist! Thank you for encouraging my "creative" side.

Nancy Newman Parker (Nance) – Who buys three white shirts at a time? You were my first friend in Fort Worth. Thank you for raising me and my family.

Mike Berry, Jim Clinkscales, Marc Epstein, John Fant, Dee Kelly, David Nichols, David Parker, Keith Parten, Chris Pruitt, Robert Self and Marshall Young – You men have two things in common. You are all married my dear friends and have all encouraged our family over many hurdles. My girlfriends have very good taste.

Mark Rice and Brian Schneider – The two men I will always think of as my adopted little brothers. Through our working relationship, we developed a true bond of trust and genuine friendship. Thank you the many computer lessons and encouragement of this project.

Mary and Tim Leake (my brother and sister-in-law) – You both have stepped up for our family. I know you will be sainted in heaven.

Maribeth and Rob Reeb – You both have been wonderful friends to our entire family. Doug and I appreciate the many times Doctor Rob helped the Woodson family...thank you.

Marilyn French Berry – Thank you for being such a good friend to the Woodson family. You are a loyal and thoughtful person.

Michelle and Tom Purvis – Your love for my family will always be appreciated. Thank you for raising Jay during his senior year!

Shari Barnes – It is hard to put in words how appreciative I am that you stood up for me with my work and education! You have inspired me to inspire all the women in this world trying to better themselves. Thank you for being my advocate and for all your support. I will be grateful to you forever.

Terry Brown Pruitt – You have always encouraged me to try new things. Your friendship has become the anchor in my daily living. Your encouragement to pray and seek God's guidance in difficult situations has been and will continue to be life saving. Thank you for believing in me. YDM

Terri Fant – You kept me sane during our children's high school years and beyond. Thank you for your friendship and calm spirit.

To my Birthday Club – Thank you!

Valerie and Michael Mallick – I am so glad our paths have crossed. Thank you for being such a wonderful support system to Jay and our family.

Veazey Krausnick and Lisa Grayson – Name two things I have learned to say (but not from my parents) - Hook'em Horns and Birth Control! You girls are the best. Thank you for supporting me through the many years.

Sherry Key – You have always believed in me. Thank you for the many opportunities and for your friendship.

Steve Sherwood – Thank you for all the support and encouragement.

Susan Young – "Talk among yourself." Linda, you just make me laugh. Thank you for all your support, generosity and love.

To my many Aunts, Uncles and Cousins – Thank you for all the love, support and encouragement to our family during the many difficult times. To this day I will never forget the many wonderful things you all did during Terry and Steve's death. I love you all.

To my many friends - I find it difficult to express my gratitude into words. Each one of you, and you know who you are raised me up in the depths of my darkness. It is your individual strength and guidance that led me through valley and I will be eternally grateful for all your love and support. "Our Friends are our Family" and they need to make me laugh. If I want to be depressed I will call my family!

To my many nieces and nephews – I am so proud of each and every one of you!

To the many doctors – Thank you!

Table of Contents

Forward

<u>Hurdles</u> is a blunt yet blistering story of my mother's battle with her illness and struggle to complete the education she postponed years ago. Even though our entire family is woven into every page, the story is told from a perspective that makes me feel as though I have never heard it at all. The details are so exquisite that I feel as if I am wearing Dorothy's red shoes.

After reading the book all the way through, I came to the conclusion that this audacious story is open to many interpretations. Hurdles started out as my mother's daily journal while she was sick, but after several unanticipated events it turned into an inspirational piece that should be shared with many. Initially, it was a story targeted to middle-aged women seeking an education, but as the story developed, it began to encompass the struggles of each member of our family.

I know that every person who reads this wonderful book will have a unique perspective of us as individuals. It is about a family who has taken the fall for its own and others' mistakes. About a mom who did what most moms would not do, she got her degree at age forty-seven. <u>Hurdles</u> written by my mother Nancy Woodson, is an inspirational memoir about a bold woman who takes no prisoners.

By Lawrence Elizabeth Woodson
Age 15

Submitted in July 2005

As I start to write this essay for admissions to the university, I am thinking about the last twelve months of my life. My journey can be compared to a long car trip with many detours and winding roads, but the destination was more beautiful than I could ever imagine. My 2005 year was a year I had been looking forward to. My oldest daughter was graduating from high school and my life was full with my family life and work at a local university. It was only the second week into January when I discovered what was to become my biggest challenge in my life. A lump in my throat proved to be thyroid cancer and for the first time in my life I was feeling like I was driving down the road only to discover a "drop off" in the path. We all have moments of fear in our life, but a fear without any control creates a panic throughout your soul. After spending a week in the hospital and learning the cancer had spread through the lymph system, I decided to adopt the phrase "mind over matter" and to face the radiation treatment with a positive attitude and self-determination. After a long six months, a clear scan revealed and I was "cancer survivor!"

My life has changed in the past twenty-years and my focus for myself has taken a new direction. My academic career and my ability to obtain my degree in the past years has been an unsuccessful journey, but through my battle of cancer I have found a new sense of determination and courage to achieve a higher education. My failure of not achieving my college degree has been the one regret I have felt for all of my adult life, and the squandering of the wasted years and money my parents have invested in me has haunted me to this day. My struggles have become my biggest blessing and I have told myself "if my cancer is not going to kill me, then I will continue my education." My disease has given me an inner strength and confidence. This has been one of the most precious times in my life. I have learned to let others help me and accept their assistance. A positive attitude can make a difference in one's life and the outcome of a crisis can be viewed as a wonderful life lesson. I am building my academic confidence slowly and telling myself to take "Take One Day at a Time." I am thrilled to think of earning a college degree and becoming alumni in the future. I constantly remind through my children that your education creates freedom and enables power. My completion of my higher learning is my lifelong desire and will be considered one of my best accomplishments. My educational journey has been a long one and at times has been taken for granted from myself.

I often compare myself to Dorothy from the Wizard of Oz. Dorothy had the capabilities to go home at anytime, but never used her full potential. I have been Dorothy through the many years searching down a yellow brick road for that one thing. My mind and desire are my red shoes and I am hoping I will find my college degree at the end of my rainbow!

Imagine the excitement and anticipation of starting the college chapter in your life; new friends, new guys, sorority rush, being on my own (as much as you could be when going to college in your home town). And then an Atomic Bomb is dropped in your lap – your **mother** is going back to school and with you. Welcome to my Hell! How could Mom do this to me, these are my four years. Why couldn't Mom let me go?

Like any selfish 19 year old I made rules Mom had to abide by while on campus; she could not acknowledge me, she couldn't eat where I did. Of course I did not take into account Mom's anxiety of becoming part of a young academic environment.

Throughout my first three years at this university my attitude toward Mom attending college with me changed very little. I have been told that throughout life there are times when out of the blue things become very clear or you figure IT out. One day my Senior year IT slapped me across the face: FAMILY is what life is all about and I was going to be the proudest graduate because Mom was a part of my graduating year.

By Bailey Woodson
Age 24

STRUGGLES BRING BLESSINGS
An Introduction

As I reflect on the last five years of my life, I often feel as if I am thinking of someone else. Through each experience, multiple life lessons have been revealed to me with many blessings and struggles. The truth is life has been overwhelming for me in recent years. To this day, it still remains devastating as I constantly tell myself to take "One Day at a Time." One of my closest friends gave me a metal door sign, with this slogan, and I immediately nailed it above my walk-in closet. I see it every day, and yet I often forget the wisdom contained in these five words. I have to remind myself to stay focused on the end goal, not on the steps that will take me there. My husband Doug, an avid sports enthusiast, calls this "keeping your eye on the ball." He tends to describe things and reflect on life with sports metaphors which mean little to me, but when I ask for his explanation, his descriptions often ring true. I often ask myself "When will life's drama end? When will I return to a calmer existence?" I have come to the conclusion that God's timing is perfect while my timing is only wishful.

Growing up in a large family (one of eight children) provided unique opportunities and numerous challenges. Logistically speaking, sharing a house with seven siblings was eventful, to say the least, and trying on a regular basis. Daily living resembled what most families experience during a family holiday. Each meal was the equivalent of an average family's Thanksgiving celebration. We managed it quite well because life in an oversized family is all we knew and if we didn't, we would experience Dad's temper as he did not tolerate any complaints or conflict at the dinner table. It was primarily through Mother's diligence, patience, firmness, and love that things ran smoothly in our household.

My mother has always been a pillar of strength for our family. A devout Catholic, she possesses a strong sense of moral responsibility and she instilled in us the virtue of right and wrong. What she taught through her faith, caring heart, and non-judgmental approach has had a tremendous impact me. With grace and style she demonstrated the utmost dedication to her husband of fifty-five years, her eight children, six children-in-law, and twenty-four grandchildren. Her family has always been the center of her life, even after my siblings and I left the nest many years ago and scattered across the country. Not a day goes by that she doesn't pick up the phone, and talk to any one of us and many times, all of us. My mother's faith has steered her through good times and bad. Her devotion to God is evident to all who know her. I aspire to be the inspirational mother she has been throughout my forty-nine years. Even though she has instilled in me so many valuable qualities, I find myself falling short of her strengths from time to time, but each day I strive to inherit her heart.

Academic work was particularly exhausting for me as a child. Throughout grade school, junior high and high school, I often had a tough time making the grade while many of my friends seemed to get through it with half the effort. Unfortunately, this pattern of struggle continued as I advanced into higher education. The academic challenges were a daily grind. Maybe this is where I first began to learn through every struggle comes a blessing. I compensated for my academic shortcomings by developing social and verbal skills. Instead of allowing my failures in the classroom to beat me down, I became quite the conversationalist and often talked my way out of several situations. Many of my "smarter" friends trembled at the thought of public speaking, negotiating or dealing with many day to day interactions, but my defense mechanisms made me "street smart" and strong in this regard, and it soon overshadowed my inferior test-taking skills.

We all have regrets in our lives. Many times these misgivings hold us back. Eventually these regrets and our inability to recognize these misgivings can start to affect our emotional and physical well-being. A true test of one's inner strength is recognizing weaknesses, acknowledging that we have regrets, and facing them head-on without fear and hesitation. Being honest to ourselves is the ultimate gift we can give ourselves. While I never gave this notion much thought in my younger days, this principle has continued to resurface throughout my adult life. What was my true desire? Where did I feel the most vulnerable and insecure? After all, I have a wonderful husband and three healthy children. Why was I feeling in the words of my high school teacher, Sister Agnes Richarda, as if I was "Selling Myself Short?" The truth is I was incredibly insecure about not having completed my college degree. My traumatic experiences of struggling in the classroom made me feel uneasy and caused hesitation about going back to college. In my mind, the obstacles of finances and physical demands presented to great a challenge for me to succeed in such a process. Fear of failure plagued me. It seemed to have its arms wrapped around me. With three children in private school and all the demands of motherhood I could easily rationalize that the timing was not right for me to go back to school. My parents provided me the opportunity for a college degree thirty plus years ago, but I was immature and didn't place much importance on it at the time. The successes I experienced during my school girl days were attributable to my personality and social skills and I was considered the "life of the party." I enjoyed the social status of obtaining an "M-r-s." degree. When I left college after four years of diligent social interaction, my friends left with their diploma, and I left with just memories. I came to the realization that social prestige is much more a perception than a reality.

Herein I pen the thoughts of my journey. I have received a special gift, the gift of understanding the true blessings in my life. Using humor as my guide, I will reveal in this memoir both my accomplishments and my struggles, and I will call this "Hurdles." Challenging me to identify and conquer my fears has been life changing. It has bolstered my self-esteem and confidence. I know that failure is always a possibility, but it is better to try and fail than never to try at all.

So here we go, as I walk you through the challenges and experiences that have turned me into the person I am today. It is my hope as you turn each page you will identify with many of my "hurdles" and come away with a new outlook in your life.

CHAPTER 1
It's Business

IT WAS THE MONDAY NIGHT of the Martin Luther King holiday that my world started to take an unexpected twist. Little did I know at the end of a relaxing three-day weekend my life would take such a dramatic and chaotic turn?

Doug, my husband, was working in the kitchen as our three children, Bailey (18 years old), Jay (15 years old), and Lawrence Elizabeth (9 years old), were in their rooms preparing for the four-day week. I was focusing on the children's schedules, while multi-tasking the packing of my travel wardrobe for a business trip the following day.

As I hurried around the house preparing for my trip, I headed down the hallway toward my bedroom. I casually placed my hand on my throat and felt an unfamiliar lump in the front of my neck. A wave of panic suddenly came over me. I quickly made my way to the full body mirror. As I peered into the glass I saw it. It was a strawberry shaped lump bulging from the right side of my throat. An uncomfortable and distressing sensation engulfed my mind and it made its way through my body. I immediately approached Doug who was seated at the kitchen table.

As his hands glided over my neck, his fingers gently returned multiple times to the swollen area. Doug closed his eyes to concentrate on his touch. He asked me how long the lump had been there. I explained that I had just then discovered it for the first time. My husband didn't seem too concerned, but he rarely displays much emotion or concern when he is initially confronted with just about anything while my anxiety and concern immediately increased. My breathing became shallow and rapid. I could feel my strong female intuition rising up inside of me increasing my fear.

I am by nature an intuitive person. My mind quickly went to the possibility that this lump was cancer. I was immediately stressed by the thought of how my children and mother would respond to the news and how it would affect them. As I stood in my room all alone it was as if I was in shock. I couldn't decide what to do next. What direction should I take? What happens now? Should I keep packing my suitcase and go about business as usual? Should I call my doctor or drive to the hospital? I felt completely overwhelmed and just stood frozen in time. Suddenly, the thought hit me I could call our next-door neighbor, Dr. William Childress. Surely he would tell me what to do so I called him and explained what I had discovered. Without hesitation he came to my house to take a look. He is direct and businesslike; I always respected him for that. I loved his approach straight to the point, honest and always accurate in his diagnosis.

I met Bill at the door and together we stepped into the dark living room. He felt the enlarged lump in my throat and immediately stated without hesitation with complete certainty, "Nancy, you have thyroid cancer." I blurted out "damn it, I knew it." I had complete trust in his opinion, I called out to Doug in a panicked voice, and he quickly appeared in the entry hall. Doug looked puzzled to see Bill standing in our home that late at night. He had a confused look on his face. I am sure he was wondering why his crazy wife had dragged this man out of his house so late in the evening.

Bill looked directly at Doug and restated his diagnosis. "She has thyroid cancer and it has to come out." Without any additional thought I blurted out, "I'm sorry, but I am leaving town tomorrow. I have 12 appointments and I have to get my numbers." My position was relatively new on the university campus and as a member of this team I was hoping to reach my upcoming one-year anniversary and becoming eligible for the tuition benefit program offered to employees and their family members. My oldest daughter, Bailey, would be entering the university as a freshman in the upcoming fall. I was carrying our family's medical insurance because it was substantially better coverage at less cost due to the fact that Doug was self-employed. My full-time employment was of major importance to our family primarily due to the benefits.

Although Doug was totally unprepared for Bill's spontaneous diagnosis, he knew he was a highly qualified medical doctor and held his opinions in high regard. His previous care and treatment of our children contributed to our confidence in his medical wisdom. Of course, I interrupted the conversation to reiterate that I had a prior commitment with twelve proven Houston prospects. Bill reassured me what I viewed as a crisis was not a life or death situation, but to consider the possibility of postponing my trip. I took a big sigh, considered his advice and thanked him for his visit as we walked him to the door.

As Doug closed the door, he turned to me and said "Let's Take One Day at a Time" and I don't think you should plan on leaving town."We mutually agreed not to talk about it until the morning. Even though it weighed heavy on our minds we didn't discuss the feared subject for the rest of the evening; however, the stress was building in our silence and body language. We agreed not to say anything to the children since the diagnosis was not yet certain even though we believed Bill was right. We were conflicted about our decision because we knew we could be concealing a life-altering matter. My future health would no doubt require inconvenient changes and potentially negative consequences for all of us.

Sleeping was a challenge that evening. Grabbing my bible and heading to the den, I entered the quiet area around four o'clock in the morning. I found myself in a totally vulnerable state. After all I am a girl that is used to being on top of things and demands control. I was feeling totally out of control with a racing mind that made me feel very uneasy.

As I was wide awake in the early morning hours, I burst into tears and cried out to God for direction and calming. The truth is I knew I had cancer. I could feel it. It was a feeling I never had or known. It was a deep, sharp, piercing pain in the core of my body. As I sat there thinking, crying, and praying I decided to face the situation with strong determination to be rational and brave. I also decided to face the cancer head on and be proactive with the process.

After I had contained my emotions and uneasiness I started going through the mail. I came across a term life insurance policy from an unsolicited mass mailing and immediately started to complete the application and by now it was 4:45 in the morning. My mind was starting to take on what I call "It's Business" attitude. It was only logical if I were unable to remain employed and provide the tuition benefit for my children, then I would provide life insurance money to cover the cost. I didn't tell Doug about this insurance policy. I completed the application filling in all the blanks with the necessary information and preparing it for mailing.

Just after 6:00 a.m., Doug entered the den. He immediately began to verbalize his thoughts and plans for the day, as I interrupted him with my own agenda to be the first unscheduled patient at the doctor's office. I explained to Doug if the doctor told me not to leave town, I would follow his direction. Additionally, if he told me I could leave; I would go ahead and fulfill my work obligation and head to Houston.

We both agreed on the plan and headed out the door at 7:30 a.m. As I left our home for the unscheduled appointment, I casually veered off direct course, heading straight to the post office where I would drop off my new financial plan. I pulled up to the mailbox and deposited the sealed envelope into the big, blue metal box. I was proud of myself for capitalizing on this opportunity. I knew if I received a cancer diagnosis, I would not be eligible for life insurance for several years.

I was the first patient in the doctor's waiting area, and I announced my presence through the glass window. When the nurse asked for my appointment time I burst into tears and explained my frightening discovery. She immediately escorted me to an empty room. Doug followed and then the doctor came in shortly thereafter.

Our internist doctor Dr. James Moore is a man of true character and a devoted family man. As Dr. Jim entered the room he immediately placed his hands around my neck while applying pressure to the thyroid area. I continued to weep while trying to explain what I had found. The doctor gripped my neck with a firm hold while pushing and feeling. He confirmed the lump and added he could feel a second lump as well. He explained more than one tumor is usually a strong indication that it is not cancerous.

As he spoke the words, I quickly interrupted him. I told him of the awful sensation inside my spirit and I felt quite sure it was cancer. He advised me that regardless of the diagnosis, the two tumors he felt should be removed in the upcoming weeks. He said I should choose a surgeon and schedule a consultation appointment. We discussed my upcoming out-of-town trip. His opinion was to continue with my plans since the test results would not be available before the weekend.

As we ended the impromptu appointment Dr. Jim offered to close my visit in prayer. I was first confused by his suggestion because I really was not sure how to interpret it. Was this his way of telling me that he thought this was very serious or that he thought I was dying? Doug thought it was wonderful and as we all held hands and prayed as I quickly decided to embrace his loving words with a calm spirit and open heart.

As we left the office, I headed to my car (we had driven separate vehicles because I intended to leave for Houston if my doctor consented.) Doug could not believe I was choosing to leave town. I kissed him goodbye, entered the driver's side of my car, and headed toward the highway. I desperately tried to stay focused on the task at hand that being my business trip, but I found it difficult to let go of the events of the past 12 hours.

It was a wonderful day to drive and escape to the open road. As the sun beamed through the haze on my windshield I loaded the compact disc with *The Phantom of the Opera* into the player and prepared my mind for some relaxing drive time. The music started and as the instruments began to play, I slowly started to feel a deep sadness. I felt as if my life was passing before my eyes and I was overcome with emotion. I cried all the way to Houston. When I arrived at my first appointment needless to say it was not a good look. I had been awake since four a.m. had little make-up on my face and had been crying for the past twelve hours. It was not one of my better looking days.

I managed to pull myself together, shift into my "It's Business" mode, and performed my duties. I parked my car, placed several eye drops in each eye and proceeded to approach the new prospect. I entered his office and immediately apologized for my tired appearance. I offered a lame excuse that the humid, Houston pollen filled air was awful on my allergies. The successful, middle-aged businessman politely made me feel comfortable about my swollen eyes and we had a very nice visit. I was on my way to a productive trip, which was a pleasant and much needed surprise given my emotional morning drive. I returned to Fort Worth four days later somewhat energized due to the productivity of the trip and the change of scenery.

I was scheduled for a sonogram the following Monday. Doug called our selected surgeon, a long-time family friend, and asked him to work me into his schedule as soon as possible. Dr. Jonathan Williams agreed to see me the next day to review the radiology films and consult us on our options.

Dr. John was the big brother of a childhood friend from Doug's neighborhood growing up. Doug had always admired him and had complete confidence in his medical expertise. The sonogram revealed three remarkable masses located on my thyroid. The three tumors were situated on the right side of the butterfly-shaped organ. Dr. John calmly reassured me by stating these tumors probably didn't contain cancerous cells. I respectfully disagreed as my mind flashed back to the day of my discovery and my next door neighbor's spontaneous diagnosis that night. I quickly apologized for being so forward, but wanted to clue him in on my strong female intuition. I turned to Doug, seeking confirmation of my comment to the surgeon, but he was unsure of the direction to take. Was he supposed to support the scared wife or the experienced physician? He suggested a needle biopsy to assess the situation but I firmly declined that option. I was convinced the tumors needed to come out and I was comfortable with this more aggressive approach. I kept thinking to myself "It's Business," I can't get emotional. I need to make the most logical, well-educated decision and then stick with it, and in my heart of hearts I felt my intuition would lead me in the right direction.

Within what seemed like seconds, a final decision was reached. The surgeon would remove the three tumors in the right cavity and test the tumors while I was still on the table for an immediate diagnosis. If the masses tested positive for cancer Dr. John would remove the entire organ and surrounding lymph nodes in hopes of extracting all of the cancerous tissue. Doug was supportive of my decision although he was uncertain if this was the best path but respected my chosen course of action.

Dr. John kindly altered his schedule for the following Monday to work me in and I prepared myself mentally for surgery. I had many things to do to get organized at home and at work. I kicked myself into "preparedness" mode knowing full well I was about to have forced R&R. After a few days I decided it was time to share the news with my mother. She immediately became upset, and both of my parents were firm on coming to town for the surgery despite my insistence that it wasn't necessary. In light of my parents' reaction, I decided that I would not inform the children until the day before the procedure. I consciously withheld from them my health information convinced it was the correct approach but that was a huge mistake, and I suspect that Doug, who is typically very pragmatic about family communication, chose to follow my lead to maintain his full support of me. I regret not communicating to my three children the potential seriousness of my condition. Despite my well-meaning intentions, my children should have been given the opportunity to voice their concerns and opinions. Their feelings were hurt and they were somewhat angered that others were informed of their mother's health before they were. I feel remorseful to this day not telling them immediately.

In the middle of all this chaos I received a phone call from a local realtor asking permission to show our house to a prospective buyer from out-of-town. This was a strange request considering the fact that our house was not currently on the market. But for the right price anything can be for sale. After all, "It's Business." If we could sell our house and make a profit why not go for it? No, it was not an ideal time, but the circumstances were not in my control. I was starting to see a pattern: there really wasn't much in my control at this point so I offered to leave him a key and told him I would be unavailable until the end of the week without disclosing the reason.

It was time to inform my boss, Susan Christy, of my upcoming surgery. Even though she was fifteen years younger, Susan had become my mentor due to her caring and professional approach to being my manager I held her in the highest regard. She was a "woman of detail" and her leadership qualities inspired me to work harder. I respected her not only as my superior, but as a friend and this was made possible by her confident, no non-sense approach. She had high expectations from her staff, but always required more from herself. She empowered me daily through her work ethic and ethical standards. Each day I strive to be a better employee because of this woman.

As I prepared for my hospital stay I felt it was important to make my home a more comfortable place. I found myself nesting in my house with new nightgowns, candles, and lotions. The pending overnight stay in the hospital would be a quick one, and I told myself my reward would be coming home to a spa environment. I felt the urge to keep my life simple to get through the days ahead. "One Day at a Time" was starting to sink in. I chose to limit my conversations to family members and a few close friends. The less said the better in my mind. I felt strongly about not receiving anyone's opinions or advice from this point forward. I knew the decisions I would make would have to be my own. I was about to venture out on a solo flight and I convinced my head I was going to be tough while my heart was scared to death. Even though I had plenty of support I would later discover just how lonely this journey would be.

CHAPTER 2
Don't Poke the Snake

THE DAY BEFORE THE SURGERY I became somewhat anxious and I asked two girlfriends to accompany me to Oak Cliff Bible Fellowship in South Dallas. It was an African American congregation, and I had always heard each service was a spiritual experience. As the three of us entered the sanctuary I felt somewhat out of place but it only took a few minutes for me to feel at ease in the affectionate church environment. The message from the preacher was very uplifting and the music was filled with emotion and extremely inspirational. The three-hour service resembled a divine revival and was nothing like the traditional Catholic service I grew up with or the Episcopalian service to which I was accustomed in my adult years. The Oak Cliff service invigorated me with a healthy mind and spirit for the days ahead. It was on this religious field trip that I first heard the singing group, the McCampbells, a family of five siblings, gospel chorus. This youthful ensemble walked onto the stage and into my life that day. I had no idea that the crossing of our paths would soon hold significance in my life and in the lives of my family. It was a wonderful day.

Doug and I left for the hospital the next day in the mid morning. I was scheduled for surgery at three o'clock in the afternoon. The children went on to school, and I told them to come by the hospital after their sports activities. I explained to the three children the doctor was going to remove a lump in my throat, but it was not anything serious. Doug and I said good-bye to each other around 1:30 in the afternoon, and I remember the lonely, agonizing wait for the nurses to come take me to surgery. The procedure was late getting started, and as I lay on the bed alone I started to doubt my seemingly aggressive decision for surgery. Once I make a decision to do something I like to do it right away. I am not the most patient person. I remembered the words of a doctor/friend who once told me: "If it grows, then it goes." My parents drove in from Oklahoma City. Doug, his mother Jo Ann, his two brothers Patrick and Chad, my parents Carolyn and Buddy and my sister Terry were all present in the hospital waiting room.

After receiving verification of cancerous cells, Dr. John immediately removed the three "complex solids" as well as the left lobe of the thyroid gland with seven surrounding lymph nodes. The surgeon described the contaminated organ as having an unusual appearance, dark in color and bone calcified. Apparently, he seemed quite surprised at the visual condition he observed.

To this day, I vividly remember my doctor standing over me in the recovery room when I asked him if it was cancer. His answer is forever etched in my mind, "You were right…it was cancer."

As word spread that the surgery time extended past the anticipated ninety minutes to four hours, family and friends whom I had told not to inconvenience themselves by coming to the hospital began to appear unannounced in the waiting room. Dr. John entered the crowded, oxygen starved area and kindly asked to speak to the "immediate" family in a nearby conference room. They all followed the surgeon into the enclosed room, anxious to receive the diagnosis. Anticipation ran high. Unaware of the surgeon's findings, my two oldest children, Bailey and Jay, casually stepped off the elevator and entered the waiting room which they later described as a "cluster." Both teenagers had finished their after school activities and driven together for a quick visit before starting their nightly academic assignments. As they walked through the crowded waiting room, they both spotted their father who was surrounded by family and friends. The host of people had taken them by surprise. They expected to see close family members only. As their eyes scanned the group, they overheard a conversation in which someone stated their mother had cancer. Jay quietly looked at Bailey and whispered, "I have to get out of here right now."

As they hurried to the elevator and into the parking lot, the children embraced each other with questioning disbelief. Why did they not know of the possible outcome of this so-called "simple" procedure? Why had the truth been shielded from them? These were fair questions. My children have asked these "why" questions over and over again. Their anger and frustration were justified. At the time, I thought it best not to alarm and worry them with the many fearful possibilities. Looking back at it I made a poor decision. I quickly realized walking through this dark valley as a family would have been a much better choice.

Bailey and Jay drove back to the house and convened by our backyard pool. Months later they shared with me their rebellious behavior on that evening. After finding out their mother had cancer in her throat Jay grabbed a cigar and Bailey her rare "social" cigarette. To this day, I still don't know if alcohol was involved, but I suspect it was for an hour and a half discussing their fears and sadness in the fact that their mom had the "C" word. Once they shared their fears and frustrations they gave each other a firm hug and were then ready to face the reality that their mother was sick and they returned to the hospital.

After the four-hour surgery and a couple hours in the recovery room, the hospital staff delivered me to my room around 8:30 in the evening. My speech was somewhat slurred and I was not very coherent, but I was alert enough to know my family and friends had packed the hospital halls as my children were nowhere to be found. Some days later I learned of their temporary lapse in judgment (although I understand it under the circumstances) before they finally graced me with their presence. Doug was emotionally exhausted. He rarely shows his feeling and tends to bottle up his emotions. I was quite surprised when my mother told me he broke down and cried when the surgeon delivered the news. I wanted him to go home with the kids and get a good night's sleep, so I accepted the offer from my mother for her to stay the night in my room.

The night was long with nurses coming in and out of the room and the pain medicine wearing off periodically. I got some sleep, but mother was awake the entire evening. A nurse entered around 2:30 a.m. to check my vitals and mental awareness by asking my name and age. My blood pressure had dipped dangerously low measuring 70 over 37. She alerted the doctor on call who was catching some shuteye while the opportunity presented itself. There was much commotion that first night after surgery. What was supposed to be one day in the hospital turned into five nights; the longest five days of my life.

As word spread through the community grapevine that I had cancer I found myself overwhelmed with the response of family and friends. I was stunned by all the cards, notes, and phone calls I received. In fact, I soon realized what an awful friend I had been to so many people over the years. So many times I felt unable to find the words to say to someone in a difficult situation, so I chose not to do or say anything at all. I would tell myself, "I'll send a card or call later when it doesn't seem so awkward," which meant I probably wasn't going to do anything at all. With that in mind, I saved every card, letter and email and would read them when I needed a boost.

On the third day after surgery I was visiting with several friends when Dr. John entered my room. He motioned for my visitors to step out as he had a serious look on his face. My mother and friends exited the room for the impromptu consultation. I was uneasy due to his demeanor as he delivered the shocking news. A lab report indicated that the cancer had grown throughout the entire thyroid and spread outside the previously thought contained area to two of the seven lymph nodes.

As I tried to process the information I burst into tears, but remained thankful that the cancerous cells were removed from my body. "The lab report was a surprise to us all," he calmly and matter of fact stated. I am forever grateful for his attention and wisdom regarding my care. I made the decision at that point I would focus on a healthy recovery, and would not let anything get in my way to accomplish this goal.

Leaving the hospital was a treat as I eagerly looked forward to crawling into my own bed, not unlike returning from a business trip or vacation; it is always with great anticipation that I yearn for my own bed. As I entered the house the magnificent aroma of fresh, cut flowers wafted from room to room. Doug had worked frantically to make sure the house looked just right upon my return, as he was clearly in a "get things done" mode. I requested some alone time to bathe and he agreed to give me some privacy and solitude on one condition: I was not to lock the door. I gingerly stepped into the bath as I soon realized shampooing my hair was going to be quite a difficult task. I sat there in those few inches of water cursing under my breath because I really wanted to wash my hair. Getting the shampoo in was easy, but getting it out was next to impossible because I could not bend my neck. Just then the bathroom door flew open and to my surprise stood two of my childhood girlfriends from Memphis. They had flown in town for the day from my hometown to visit their sick friend. What a blessing and treat this turned out to be.

As I was sitting naked in the tub the immediate awkwardness of the moment evaporated with their reaction to an elective surgery I had a few years prior. Taken by surprise and feeling somewhat undressed, I quickly issued an edict: If they were going to interrupt my bath time then they would have to wash my hair. We all had a good laugh as they washed my hair removing all the shampoo and then these precious friends placed my old robe on my tired, weak body. As I started to tear up at the way they had just cared for me they teased me because my favorite, old terry cloth robe was sporting several holes. I loved my old robe and planned to keep it until it disintegrated from all the washing machine trips.

The three of us piled up onto my bed as if we were in high school again and watched the movie *When Harry Met Sally*. It was wonderful to have that time alone with two of my best old friends. After all, "Old Friends are the Best." Two weeks later, I received a care package from them with a new pink, fluffy robe.

The Robe

The robe with the holes brings joy to my heart
for it reminds me of friends traveling together not apart
the new gift was cozy and lifted my day
but the old one was more familiar and I chose it to stay
with the two hanging in the bathroom side by side
every day I would choose the old and wear it with great pride
new can be exciting but old has more appeal
the memories warm me up with love and make everything seem so real

February 12, 2005

During my first week home from the hospital a realtor returned with a prospective buyer from out of town for a second showing. I proudly gave them a tour in my pajamas. The house was disorganized and not very clean as we stepped over many items left on the bedroom floors by all three children. I escorted the potential buyer through Jay's room and apologized for the sleeping teenager in the bed. He was exhausted from a grueling high school poker game the night before. I requested forgiveness for the condition and appearance of my home and they kindly apologized for requesting a second showing so soon after my hospital stay. I reassured them it was not a problem primarily because I was pleasantly enjoying the "party" going on in my head as a result of all the pain medication.

After two weeks of staying home I decided to venture out and go to the office to get some fresh air and test my stamina. I was very weak and tired, but I knew it was best for my mental health to get out of the house and into the real world. I thought getting dressed and putting on some lip-gloss would point me in the right direction of a healthier state of mind. I was very self-conscious of the huge scar on my neck, but when I added a fashionable scarf, I felt much better and found my sense of humor returning.

The truth is I was scared to death, but at the same time I felt strong. This didn't make sense although fear can be a strong motivator. I was taking "One Day at a Time" and coaching myself to stay positive. Over the previous weeks I spent more time by myself than ever before. I never knew how much I appreciated my alone time to reflect, pray and consider where my life had taken me. Painful headaches frequently prevented me from verbal conversations, so I found myself learning and loving the art of writing.

Writing was a wonderful way for me to become more aware of my feelings and surroundings and enabled me to communicate my discoveries. For once I was able to speak my mind with the love of words and their meanings. It was a form of communication I had never embraced due to the many bad experiences in the classroom, but I was beginning to enjoy my newfound ability to express an idea in my mind by translating it into words on paper. I never knew how mentally deep I could go. Sometimes I would get lost in my thoughts as I expressed myself in print. Writing my feelings, combined with the fear of the unknown, was a wonderful way to share my thoughts with myself. I was able to connect my mind and body together by using creative language as I abandoned any concern for punctuation, grammar and sentence construction that dogged me with stress throughout school. I just let it rip and I found this to be therapeutic. Processing my life through writing has been healing to my soul!

Valentine's Day was fast approaching and I decided it was a wonderful time and opportunity to thank everyone for the many flowers, cards, inspiring notes, gifts and meals. Lawrence, my ten-year old daughter and I decided to make a card expressing our love and appreciation. Lawrence crafted the design and I created the poem. Together we colored and placed glitter on each of the 250 cards as it redirected the "cancer" conversation to a fun and creative activity.

Our Friends are Our Family

Our Friends are Our Family
I have discovered this to be true
with the many flowers, meals, visits and cards
makes a recovery very manageable, and inspires me to say thank you
through every "struggle" comes a "blessing"
with the feel of God's grace
it has been the love and support of family and
friends and seeing everyone's smiling face

February 14, 2005

For the first time in forty-four years I could see my life taking another direction. I was discovering something new about myself. Taking the time to reflect and write contributed to this new direction. How could it be that I did not know everything about me? After all I should know myself better than anyone since I have spent so much time with myself.

The truth is we must open ourselves up to new things in hopes of discovering an unknown love. Unless we try new things, we will never know our full capabilities or unrecognized passions in our hearts and minds. Pushing me to "step out of the box" and write down my thoughts was uncharted territory. I had never expected this type of joy and contentment from myself. After several attempts at late night poems and journal entries I once again saw God's hand in my life.

There were some days emotionally better than others, and I knew this would be the case. My boss gave me a list of ten job responsibilities.

Number one on the list, beat cancer! She walked into my office one day handed me the typed memo, and immediately released the daily pressure of my job expectations. She told me I should take it slow and start off with ninety minutes a day and build from there. She would constantly remind me if I had overstayed my welcome and when it was time to head home for my afternoon rest. The short work day combined with getting dressed and going to work every day, was very healthy for my mind, attitude and recovery.

Attitude

A positive attitude makes a world of difference
and can turn things around
it can face opposition
and never let you down
you see things clearer in a whole new light
it keeps your mind in focus during the middle of the night.
A positive prayer life helps you hear the word of God
your life will receive His direction, instead of listening to your I-pod

February 21, 2005

Because of the lack of thyroid hormone at times I could feel my mood starting to swing. Sadness would overcome me. I had never felt such waves of depression and hopelessness. I knew this temporary state was part of my recovery, and I had to remind myself to stay positive. I would tell myself after the radiation therapy that I would be able to start the thyroid medication and regain my normal feeling and disposition. My husband often commented on how he wished he could invent an alarm that would go off when my levels were off.

When my mood was not changing and my head not hurting I started to notice a strange pain in my left shoulder. The simple task of lifting a glass of water was an excruciating experience. I was very confused as to why I was having this ache. I even wondered if someone had pulled my arm back during my operation. After all it didn't hurt before the surgery and now out of the clear blue I couldn't lift my arm above my head. I thought that maybe I just laid on it funny while I was sleeping or maybe was just the aging process at work on my body.

The next six weeks would be the most challenging of all. The thyroid replacement medications were not allowed until all remaining thyroid hormones had exited my body. In order for the treatment to be successful all thyroid levels would need to be non-existent. Otherwise, the radioactive iodine therapy would be ineffective. The thyroid gland has so many functions in the body; I had no idea of all things such a small organ impacts. It controls the body's thermostat; controls mood swings, affects memory while regulating the body's metabolism.

According to my doctor once the treatment was completed the thyroid replacement therapy would begin, consisting of one small pill per day.

Bodies

Our bodies are a mystery
a product of His might
a temple of perfection
an everyday delight
we take each day for granted
and treat it with such dismay
only when we face turmoil
do we constantly try not to stray
our bodies are the product of our everyday life
may we turn each day into His glory and honor His delight

February 28, 2005

Not being able to start the thyroid medication would mean all levels would plummet and my sanity could be called into question. I love how my new endocrinologist gently cautioned my husband about the weeks ahead. "Turn a deaf ear and walk out of the room, Doug. Whatever you do, don't react to her and her comments. She is getting ready to take on multiple personalities, imagine PMS times one hundred." At this moment Doug reiterated his desire to create his "smart ass" hormone level invention.

Doug and I had no idea what the doctor was talking about, but within a few short weeks we understood completely. The irrational mood swings often took over my body. I would recite the same statement or ask the same question to my husband over and over again. "Don't Poke the Snake," was my code phrase to leave me the hell alone...... I am going crazy in my head.

CHAPTER 3
Our Friends are Our Family

I WAS THRILLED TO HAVE SOMEONE interested in the house, but the thought of actually selling and physically moving was not in my realm of thinking at this time. The walls of our house had become confining and were closing in on our growing children who desired additional space and more privacy. I was thrilled to think of a new house with more room. However, in my mind I viewed this as just another tire kicker wasting our time, but in reality I now had some extra time to waste.

It was my fifth week on this crazy thyroid-free ride and the pain was very intense due to the dwindling hormone levels in my body. The simple act of supporting my head in an upright position had become a painful chore. Most foods were unappealing with the exception of milk and ice cream. Foods that I previously enjoyed and often craved were of no interest. I experienced continual nausea causing rapid and noticeable weight loss, as I started to take on a frail appearance. I found it difficult to talk on the phone so emailing on my blackberry became my primary method of communication.

My sweet friends constantly brought meals, knowing my family had to eat as I was not up to it. It was Bailey's senior year of high school and the combined stress of all the senior activities and having a sick mother was starting to take its toll on her. I sensed she felt somewhat cheated out of the senior experience because the focus was on my health issue and now trying to sell our home instead of her graduating accomplishments and activities. She rarely complained, but I could see the disappointment in her eyes.

The children's schoolwork was quite demanding as Doug stepped up and consistently assisted Lawrence with her daily lessons. Doug was proud to have our three children at his alma mater even though the financial burden was heavy. This private school had become a part of the Woodson tradition with a combination of 43 years of learning between Doug, Bailey, Jay and Lawrence. Having two children in high school proved challenging with all the weekend social activities, but having a fourth grader also proved challenging during the academic week. Schoolwork had always been a challenge for Bailey and Lawrence, but Bailey being eight years older had developed coping skills like her mother. Lawrence's teacher suggested testing her for a potential learning disability and we thought if we were going to test one child, maybe we should test both girls. Bailey had been at her school for fourteen years (first grade twice) and during that time never once had a teacher or administrator suggested she be tested in order to potentially qualify for additional time during test taking. Only after she was unable to complete the timed sections on the SAT college entrance exam did we realize there was a problem.

During my recovery Doug and I received both girls' test scores, which included detailed and specific reports. According to the testing expert both girls had similar learning styles and both girls qualified for additional time for all testing. The extra time could not benefit Bailey with her high school curriculum or her college admission process because this discovery came too late, but could be beneficial to her college career. Doug and I were upset as to why this type of testing was never suggested to us during her fourteen-year career by any of her previous teachers.

We made an appointment with the headmaster of our school, Dickson Short. Our previous conversations with Dickson had been limited to small talk of no substance, and this was our first time to ever discuss a consequential concern. We wanted answers as to why our daughter had gone through this exclusive college preparatory school that prides itself on offering such wonderful academic opportunities and our daughter had gone all the way through with unrecognized learning challenges.

We entered Dickson's office and promptly expressed our frustration with our daughter having fallen through the cracks of the system. The informal discussion quickly developed into a heated exchange.

As he started to make excuses for the school's oversight, I became irritated with his condescending demeanor. Bailey was not graduating as one of the highest scoring students (her standing placed her in the bottom twenty-five percent in a class filled with exceptional students), but at the end of the day the weaker students should be treated with equal opportunity.

I boldly stated: "This school doesn't give a rat's ass about the average child, and it makes me mad that we have spent so much time, energy, and money on this campus and no one detected or told us she should be tested for a learning disability." Dickson quickly became defensive and his voice increased in volume. He explained how his own child had experienced limited success in the academic world, yet had become a thriving young man. He bragged how he pulled for the weaker student as he had experienced it personally as a parent.

Dickson never accepted responsibility or apologized for the school's failure to recognize Bailey's learning challenges. Our mission in informing him was to illustrate what we saw as a trend that the school was focusing on the top students at the expense of the average student exposing a weakness in his administration, but we were unsuccessful. He offered to speak with the Dean of Admissions of her desired college as a positive recommendation and the meeting ended. Little did I know the damage my comment would cause my family that day. Losing my temper proved to be problematic for Lawrence in the years to come.

Doug's mother had just completed knee replacement surgery that required an intense recovery regimen with three weeks in a rehabilitation facility. Jo Ann's three boys and husband were all present for the surgery and multiple visitations while she was bed ridden. Until one day, Doug visited her and came away concerned from their conversation due to her slurred words and confused state. After an immediate consultation, it was discovered that she had suffered a mild heart attack, but would regain a complete recovery. She completely understood the serious nature of her condition, followed doctor's orders and with hard work and determination was soon walking with a new, stronger knee.

I was quite anxious about the upcoming radioactive iodine treatment. I knew the faster I completed the treatment, the faster I would be able to start with the thyroid medications and return to being an emotionally sound person.

Our house surprisingly had become a hot commodity as two

contracts were in competition to be the winning bid and it sold within a few weeks. Here we did not even have our home of fourteen years on the market, but I was confident selling it was the right thing to do even though the timing was not ideal.

The six week wait had finally arrived come and it was time for the much anticipated radiation iodine treatment. Doug and I entered the hospital for my one-night stay and were escorted to the lobby and instructed to wait for my name to be called. According to the admittance personal, the sterile, "plastic covered" room was not yet available. It wasn't until we entered the room that we understood why it took so long to prepare the space. Four hours later and battling a tremendous migraine headache, I entered the "bubble" room. The nurse reminded me that anything I took into this miniature compound would be left behind following treatment and disposed of for fear of radioactive contamination. With a great deal of thought I carefully chose a few items. What was cheap and would hold my interest for more than a day? Magazines, Chap Stick, and bobby pins made the list. These items became of utmost importance in my immediate universe. Doug listened intently as the rules and instructions of the restricted stay were recited by the nurse. "Flush the toilet three times after each use, run the water for five minutes after brushing your teeth or washing your hands." Doug was somewhat freaked out by the extent of the sterile environment, where we kissed goodbye and he returned home. I could tell he was mystified by the plastic covered living conditions. He quickly exited the room with the few items of clothing I removed to put on the hospital gown.

Over the next weeks I felt more bold and confident. My battery was starting to recharge with a positive outlook and spring in my step. In my mind, battling my illness became an accomplishment never a punishment. I never felt anger with God, quite the opposite. I was grateful for his love and for the care I had received from the many family members, friends and doctors. These people had lifted me up and took me under their wing. For the first time in my life, I was forced to let others do for me and give up the control. God was teaching and reminding me once again it was about His timing, not mine. I was astounded by the affection of those around me. My illness has taught me to put myself out there and take more chances with myself. Cancer strengthened my confidence to embrace life and the many wonderful opportunities it has to offer. Daring ourselves to learn, love and live is the ultimate gift we can give ourselves. I received a bold reminder that our time on this earth is limited. I have been given an opportunity to do more for others and make the most out of every moment I live. What a gift!

I could hear the sound of the starting gun and see the drop of the colorful flag. I was nervous with my first "baby" steps but excited to start the race.

I continue to stand amazed at this journey on which God is taking me on. In fact, I picture Him gently smiling as I am humbled again and again. I know He must shake His head often as he watches my day-to-day struggles. I'm sure He utters, "Oh Nancy, my precious child, you are learning and growing." Sometimes I catch myself skipping down the figurative yellow brick road with a basket full of "my ways." I seem to focus on "my way" of doing things and "my way" of dealing with circumstances. God reminds me by doing this I continue to "sell myself short" and close myself off to a more infinite approach to life's hurdles that can only come from Him.

CHAPTER 4
Forced Family Fun

AFTER STAYING HOME FOR ANOTHER five days, I was ready to put the whole experiences behind me. Starting the new thyroid medication was a welcome daily ritual I could not wait to embrace. I knew my sound mind would return shortly and my family would soon feel it unnecessary to leave the room whenever I entered. I knew deep in my heart they would want to spend time with me. They might even want to engage in a stimulating conversation with me as long as I did not overreact or freak out.

My hopes were dashed. The medicine did not live up to the hype. The medicine actually took weeks to enter my system and until then the headaches continued. The pain was intense and the slightest noise elevated the ache. Without speaking a word my eyes revealed my misery and my demeanor revealed the hurt.

Another big challenge was achieving a good night's sleep. I found myself physically exhausted, as sleep became a stranger to me. It was the strangest feeling. I was too tired to keep my eyes open and at the same time too awake to sleep. I would begin the day so completely drained that I felt like I was losing my mind. I started using a nightly sleeping aid and with the assistance of a little blue pill, I finally got some rest and managed to function throughout the day.

Spring break was upon us and the "famous senior class trip" (or the "infamous" depending on who you asked) was approaching. I was dreading this teenage "heaven" in Mexico, but Doug and I decided to endure the misery together. Our last scheduled event before leaving town was attending Jay's baseball tournament. We planned to spend Saturday at the ballpark and then board the plane for some "forced family fun" the next day. Game day weather was beautiful. Jay, a sophomore at that time, was excited to play in his first varsity tournament. We did not realize at the time that God was once again preparing us for another life lesson.

We were cheering on the team, and I can still remember to this day exactly where we sat in the third base line bleachers. I answered a cell phone call from another senior mother planning to pontificate about the upcoming "pain train" senior class trip to Mexico. The conversation caught me by surprise. Doctors had recently diagnosed her father with cancer, and he had just suffered a setback. I admired her father as he was in top physical condition and participated in multiple physical adventures. He climbed mountains all over the world, ran marathons and was determined to conquer physical challenges. My friend began to share the details of her father's setback. As I sat silently on the other end of the line, I experienced an overwhelming emotional moment. My tears began to flow over a man I had rarely spoken to. What was that all about? I think I subconsciously felt that if he was having a hard time then maybe I was next. She immediately sensed my fear and anxiety and interrupted my breakdown. She firmly told me to pull myself together. She said her father would be fine. Her father died three months later.

My outburst shocked me. I didn't realize this deep-rooted fear was lurking in the shadows of my soul. This was a defining moment in my life. It was the first time I truly grasped that I had cancer. I was the girl with cancer. In my head I knew it, I had heard the doctor say it, but until now I had not felt it. I had just been going through the systematic process and had not emotionally connected with the feelings deep inside. I was so focused on feeling better and nourishing my scar with vitamin E that I had not thought about the long-term maintenance of having "the big C." My friend reminded me to stay positive and we said our goodbyes. When I ended the call I had no clue what was coming down the pike next. In just a few minutes our family would be faced with another "hurdle" in our life. This time it was Jay.

Jay stepped up to the plate for his turn at bat his forceful swing made full contact with the ball for a solid base hit. As he headed toward first base at top speed, he heard a pop, followed by sharp, intense pain in his right knee. Doug and I could see the anguish in his face and his stride immediately took on a different rhythm. The inning ended with Jay on third base and when he reached the dugout the trainer immediately applied ice to the tender area, but it offered little relief. At least the timing was good. Leaving town for spring break provided the perfect opportunity to rest the knee. A week on the beach would give the injured knee time to heal; at least that was what we thought. Little did we know that Jay was about to get some very bad news and learn a life lesson of his own.

I was packing for the famous senior trip. I just couldn't believe I was going or that I had to go for that matter. Part of me wanted to stay home alone; but I had been alone so much that staying home by myself for another week did not appeal to me. Of course going to the beach with 65 high school seniors and a few families didn't really do it for me either. We decided as a family that I was to go and I continued to pack. I fondly and kiddingly refer to family outings as F3… "Forced Family Fun!"

An F3 usually starts out as a normal family outing. Then, out of the blue, conditions can advance to a more hazardous condition known as an F4. Here's where you have to be careful. Without warning adverse circumstances can suddenly take over any family gathering and the result is an F5, which can be devastating.

F3 – Forced Family Fun
F4 – Forced Family Frickin' Fun
F5 – The Real Deal

While in Mexico, Doug pulled his weight and then some with the children patrolling the nightly teenage scene. He entertained our youngest daughter, Lawrence (age 10) at the local water parks during the day to allow me some quiet time. He graciously sent his healing wife to the adult beach with a book and my iPod shuffle for some solitude and relaxation. It was calming to look out into the water, watch the waves, while listening to my favorite tunes. Until then I didn't know one could actually listen to the "quiet." What a gift. The beach is such a peaceful place for me. I felt my spirit and body being restored as I sat in the warm breeze.

The Mexican nightlife was not desirable to one with tired eyes and massive headaches. The evenings offered a different pace and retiring early was the perfect ending to a perfect day. Taking the time to nourish one's spirit is the secret to success.

I was glad to wrap up the week of Forced Family Fun. As the five-day excursion came to an end, I remember walking through the airport and feeling as though I had not slept for weeks. I was returning from a semi-relaxing vacation only to feel more tired and exhausted than I did before the trip started. The radiation treatment, combined with a day of traveling and spending each day in the sun made me weak and tired. The prospect of walking into the house to loads of laundry was difficult to think about. With the spring break trip behind me, I could check off another task on my "to do" list. I had multiple things to complete within the next thirty days including finding a new home. Thank goodness the senior trip was behind us and having survived the mandatory excursion behind us was a huge relief.

Waiting to have my first scan in six months was agonizing. It was testing my patience – one of my weakest areas. I just wanted to skip ahead and be done with it. I was tired of discussing the last seven weeks and just wanted to be a normal person without any drama. Instead we had a mother/wife with cancer, a graduating senior and now a house move. Needless to say this was a stressful time for our family.

Being faced with the task of finding a new home was challenging, and now had become a reality. I told myself everything would work out and I just had to trust that God would provide what we needed. I must confess, not knowing what my health situation would be in six months made me very nervous. If I were looking at more surgery the thought of renovating a house was overwhelming. There were only twenty-four hours in a day. Working full time and raising three children while being sick was starting to freak me out a little. I knew I was ready to sell our home so as a group we made a conscious decision to be sensitive to each other during this adventurous time.

One of my favorite houses became available in our neighborhood and I immediately asked Doug to consider it for our family. The house had immense charm but would require a considerable amount of updating. Doug and I had never renovated a home before, and the thought of the future time commitment made us both question if we had lost our minds, considering the craziness that already existed in our life. However, after much discussion and debate, we decided to make an offer and move forward on what I thought was our dream home.

Doug prepared a contract and was ready to submit our offer. In the meantime, I received a phone call from a friend. She informed me of a home for sale in her neighborhood. The area was on the other side of town and only a few miles from the children's school. Intrigued, I felt compelled to explore her referral. I called Doug at Jay's baseball game and asked him to meet me at the newly listed house.

When we walked into the house, we were pleasantly surprised. The house was new, in immaculate condition and with only a few cosmetic changes would be perfect for our family. Doug and I slowly walked through the house, and I remember looking at him and saying "Oh man…it's perfect!" Doug replied, "Do we want to leave our neighborhood and all our friends?" Our emotions were mixed. There must be a reason for a new location but we were not sure what the reason would be. It would only be later that we would come to understand our journey. It is amazing how God has His hand in our lives! I do wonder why I fight it 24/7. I have total access to His greatness, yet I would rather try to do it myself - the hard way, the wrong way. Just like Dorothy heading down the yellow brick road, I am choosing the long and winding path.

We thanked the owners for opening their home to us and for their time. We went back to our house for a glass of wine and a discussion on what to do next. As evening was drawing to an end, Bailey and Jay returned home from their high school activities. We told them about viewing another home across town as they both expressed a desire to move closer to their school. The kids were both in agreement that it was time to exit our neighborhood of fourteen years and take advantage of a new adventure. Their input caught me off guard and I quickly realized their logic was not totally unreasonable. After all, the last few months had been chaotic and certainly unplanned. My health issue had caused us to rethink taking on a home renovation at this time. There was something exciting about a new home in a new neighborhood and leaving behind the stressful situation.

Doug and I felt compelled to listen to our children's request. We decided to see it as a sign that it was time for something different. It was time to branch out and step "out of the box." Moving to the other side of town would be a totally different direction for our family and out of character. On the other hand, it was refreshing to think of something out of the ordinary. It was not in my makeup to "color outside the lines," but I discovered that I needed to let go the desire to control everything and just go with the flow. If something was tugging at my heart to make this move maybe this was God's way of telling me to try something new.

It was a mutual and unanimous family decision to move across town to an unfamiliar neighborhood and we embraced our new home that required few demands. The timing of this home transition had one glitch, as the sellers could not vacate the property for two months due to construction delays on their new home. Doug and I decided to make best of it so we stored almost all of our belongings and moved into a three story apartment complex for the two months. Little did we know how problematic the multiple levels would be in the upcoming weeks? Obstacles seemingly just kept coming our way and found these latest events as another "hurdle" in our adventurous life.

Maybe moving to a more secluded neighborhood would allow me to focus on my family and me. All of my friends were amazing during my surgery and recovery, but in truth I felt overwhelmed. The attention I received through meals and visits was marvelous, but often exhausting. Maybe I could get a bike and enjoy the beautiful bike trails in the new neighborhood. Maybe I should embrace this new adventure and go full force. Wait. The thought of me in bike shorts was a bit scary.

CHAPTER 5
You Can't Prove That

JAY'S KNEE PAIN PERSISTED SO we took him to the doctor and an X-ray revealed of a fracture in his kneecap with cartilage damage and bone degeneration. Dr. George Underhill, an orthopedic surgeon, recommended immediate surgery due to the severity of the condition and to hopefully allow adequate recovery time to play football his junior year. Jay always enjoyed playing baseball but his true love was playing football. Preparing Jay for knee surgery did not involve much effort because we had little time to prepare. Dr. Underhill concluded a bone graft was required to replace dead bone within the knee. A MRI revealed a previous injury had caused an interruption of blood flow to a portion of his right knee. The resulting lack of oxygen caused a portion of the bone to die directly in the middle of his kneecap. I felt like once again our family was being tested with another "hurdle." I was just trying to survive and continue moving forward through the motions of life. My headaches were still present; as I felt sure my thyroid medicine was not adjusted correctly.

Jay's surgery did not go as smoothly as expected. Additional dead bone was discovered during the procedure; quite a bit more than the surgeon anticipated. The doctor updated us hourly with details of the procedure, but it wasn't until after the surgery that he told us that due the extent of the repair that Jay's knee would require a full twelve months to recover, allowing for the complete regeneration of the bone. The surgery took almost four hours and consisted of a plug of Jay's tibia being cut out and the extracted bone pummeled into a mushy consistency that was then packed into the dead bone tissue area and held together with metal screws. Waiting for bone to grow is like watching paint dry. It is a slow and boring process that requires a lot of patience.

The news shocked me and devastated Doug. Jay's junior football season was not to be. Doug knew the impact this would have on his son and the thought of Jay's reaction to the news was heartbreaking. All this happened on the coattails of my illness, his grandmother's heart attack and a house move.

After the doctor concluded his unanticipated prognosis I turned to Doug and could see the heartbreak in his face. We knew this would be a difficult time for our son. With his father as his coach Jay started playing football when he was in 5th grade and everything they worked for was to culminate in a successful high school career and now one of his two most important seasons was gone. Even in our moments of disappointment, we were so grateful that we were not faced with a life-threatening situation with our child. However, to a sixteen year old football player this was devastating. We both sat still in the sad moment, when I suddenly leaped to my feet and snarled, "You are more upset about Jay not being able to play football than you were about me having cancer." He slowly lifted his head and with a slow, deliberate tone replied, "You Can't Prove That."

Doug planned to leave town the following day for an annual convention in Las Vegas. He was confident he would take his trip until he walked into the recovery room and saw his son's condition. Doug was taken aback by the physical state of his son. He could not lift his leg. Going to the bathroom was a tremendous struggle. Jay only requested help from his father. It relieved me from nurse duty and put my husband on 24/7 patrol. By this time, we realized Doug's trip would not happen, as he would have to stay home to care for his temporarily immobilized son.

We were a few weeks into the three-story condo where Jay was "recovering" in what we fondly called the "closet" next to the kitchen on the second level of a three-story unit, with the shower on the third floor. Even though this confinement was to last only two months it felt like an eternity during this extended and more difficult recuperation time. The daily routines of life, such as bathing and eating had become complicated. What should have taken only seconds turned into hours to complete the simplest of tasks. The only up-side to this calamity was the license he received to skip school and become a video game master.

I found myself going in multiple directions before each sunrise. It was an early morning race to administer Jay's pain medicine, prepare his breakfast, and arrive to work before eight o'clock. So much for being off nurse duty as Lawrence had only a few weeks of school left before the summer. Bailey, the graduating senior, had concluded her classes sleeping until the early afternoon. And to add to the madness, we were preparing to move again into our new house. I found myself going into the storage area to just stare at the hundreds of boxes and feeling a wave of uneasiness consume me. There it was; my entire life packed into multiple boxes condensed into a 60 by 60 space.

Bailey's high school graduation was finally here and we were all very excited to see her receive her well-deserved diploma. I was thrilled at the thought of watching my first-born walk across the grand stage to receive her recognition. I decided to treat myself to a new dress and shoes to celebrate the occasion. The afternoon of shopping had concluded as I headed back to the condo to prepare for the evening celebration. Suddenly, Bailey entered the apartment in a total panic. She was tired and stressed from the multiple festivities leading up to the big night and the thought of it all coming to an end seemed to overwhelm her. As she opened her closet door she quickly became frustrated with her existing wardrobe and burst into tears. I ran into my bedroom, grabbed my new dress and shoes and handed her the outfit. She immediately looked at me and through her tears said, "Mom, you bought that for yourself, not me." I replied, "You Can't Prove That." She threw her arms around me and thanked me for the dress. It fit her perfectly, and I proudly wore the same church clothes from the weekend before.

The hour prior to the ceremony included helping Jay with his first outing since the surgery. It had to be the hottest day of the year. Doug was in a dress suit and was practically dressing Jay while guarding his lame knee. He told everyone to sit tight as he drove around the corner to pick up his mother, who was recovering from her knee replacement combined with a mild heart attack, both of which had occurred in the past three months. Doug wanted her to enter a cool-air-conditioned car and not fight the 108-degree Texas heat. He returned to the condo parking lot with his mother sitting in the cool automobile. Doug then escorted Jay down the flight of steps to the parked car. This was his first adventure since his surgery and he was thrilled to get out of our cramped living quarters. What should have been a five-minute transport turned into a 45-minute ordeal. Doug was exhausted after three steps, as he quickly realized he had grossly misjudged the complexity of this maneuver. Standing Jay to his feet and balancing him down the steep stairs sounds relatively easy, but the combination of his body size (6'3" 245 lbs) and his casted leg made this task quite difficult. With sweat rolling down both of their foreheads, Jay carefully protected his right leg with care and in full determination endured the pain of the first few steps.

Drenched with perspiration and frustrated, father and son finally approached the car. Doug carefully placed Jay in the front seat. He started to shut the door but quickly discovered the impossibility of this seating arrangement. The stiff leg in its fully bandaged contraption would not allow the car door to close. We all stood in silence observing the situation; with the exception of Mrs. Woodson who was comfortably relaxing in the air-conditioned automobile. Doug calmly suggested we relocate Jay to the back seat. Lawrence and I lifted our fancy dresses and flew over the second seat towards the third seat. In that moment, we all wondered why Jay was attempting to attend his sister's graduation, while in such a challenging physical condition. The question in everyone's mind was is this actually going to happen and get him to his sister's graduation?

As we pulled up to the coliseum entrance, we realized that we had just traveled half a mile and it took us an hour to do it. We were all exhausted.

With graduation behind us, preparing Bailey for her freshman year in college was another assignment I was starting to embrace many additional tasks. Multiple sorority recruitment packets were due in two weeks and I also had to wrap and deliver about thirty graduation gifts. I was feeling somewhat overwhelmed, but once again I told myself to break it down into "Baby Steps" and just take it "One Day at a Time." I constantly coach myself through the panic of overload to break down the chores into small manageable tasks. I reminded myself at the start of each day: anything that didn't get done that day would still be there tomorrow.

Work was moving along and my travel schedule had still been placed on hold since before my cancer surgery in January. Susan, my boss was amazing and her genuine concern for my physical well-being was deeply appreciated. It motivated me to work harder and smarter. I knew I had to stick to the physical boundaries I had set for myself and listen to my body in order to remain productive.

The pain in my left shoulder had become persistent. Even the simple task of lifting a glass of water had become painful. Whenever I lifted my arm up into the air, I would feel an unspeakable twinge that would shoot throughout my body and literally take my breath away. The pain left me totally confused. What was going on? Why was I having yet another physical challenge? I decided to meet the pain head on.

I made an appointment with Jay's knee doctor Dr. Underhill, to determine the cause of the pain in my right shoulder. He immediately ordered several tests and concluded it was scar tissue in my rotator cuff was the culprit. His thoughts were that it was probably the result of an old injury as he prescribed multiple physical therapy sessions and believed the exercises would relieve the immediate pain.

Jay and I were quite a pair, traipsing down to the medical district for our rehabilitation therapy sessions. He still could not drive, so it was a true family effort to arrange his transportation to the many doctor appointments and multiple rehab sessions. Most of his peers were participating in the summer football workout program at school and he was finding it difficult to stay positive while fighting sadness and anger.

CHAPTER 6
One Day at a Time

THE SUMMER WAS IN FULL swing after moving into our new home. I was finally starting to feel some relief. I had hopes of returning to a calmer life. The move had exhausted me with far too many packed boxes waiting to be emptied. I pretended to myself that I was opening Christmas gifts to make the grueling chore a little more exciting. It was a thrill to reconnect with my many of my "favorite things" that I had not seen in quite some time such as pictures, knick-knacks, decorative crosses and collectibles.

It was a brief yet emancipating experience to have lived a simpler life during those few months of apartment living. No frills, just the bare essentials. However; I found it comforting to arrange my many sentimental items. I have come to realize I am spending my adult life collecting items that could be worthless to others but simply make me happy.

After a few days in our new home, I returned to the orthopedic doctor for a follow-up visit. I was still experiencing pain in my left shoulder. It wasn't responding to the physical rehabilitation regimen I was religiously following three times a week. Dr. Underhill gave me the option to continue with physical therapy and much to my surprise, he offered a more aggressive treatment option. He recommended a surgical procedure that would remove the aging scar tissue in my left rotator cuff, which he believed was the culprit that was causing my pain. Mentally and physically I was not prepared for another surgery although the pain warranted the procedure. My body was just beginning to recover from the thyroid surgery I had four months prior.

The thought of an immediate "fix" was appealing. I was feeling pressured at work because of my previous sick leave. Going to the medical district two to three times a week for rehabilitation, working full time, managing three children and a husband was starting to wear me out. So once again I found myself shifting into the "It's Business" mode and I opted for the more aggressive approach.

Again my husband was not convinced that this was the best path, but was very supportive. Now that I had learned my lesson and gotten my children involved they too were questioning my decision. They did not realize how unbearable the pain was at times. I continued to recite the doctor's words in my mind: "Nancy, it is not normal at age 44 not to be able to lift your arm above your head."

We had been down this road before. I had much to do to prepare for another surgical procedure. I stocked our refrigerator and pantry with food for the upcoming week and arranged fresh flowers throughout the house. I restocked my "spa" collection of candles, lotion, and bubble bath to reinforce that comfortable feeling that I had come to desire during uncertain times.

I had never really understood or truly appreciated the flower thing in the past, but after receiving so many flowers and plants after my cancer surgery, I decided that flowers are a wonderful gift to share with others and yourself. The scent and beauty of fresh flowers made me smile and gave me strength. I had received so many beautiful arrangements in January and I loved the variety of vases that held them. I previously thought fresh flowers were wasteful because of their limited life span. My health had caused me to contemplate and appreciate things that I had previously given little thought to. I was learning to embrace the moment and smell the roses.

I started to doubt my aggressive approach and question my decision to have the surgery because I just didn't have time for my body not to work. In the end, I knew it was the right decision for me and my family, so I stood firm in my choice. After all, I had so much at stake with the job benefits, I had to move forward and be strong.

The shoulder procedure was surprisingly routine and once again I found myself embracing the forced R&R. Doug waited on me with a loving heart just as he had in the previous months. He prepared many meals for the family, drew my bath and turned down my bed each night.

My second surgery was a success and I returned to work the following Monday, but I opted to forgo the large, confining pillow sling. I just couldn't answer all the health questions at work again, so I casually dangled the sore arm to my side. The stitches remained for ten days with covered bandages no one could see. The less said the better.

CHAPTER 7
That Is Not Appropriate

Bailey's senior year with months of social activities had finally concluded as we redirected our focus to her heading off for college. The hot summer consisted of shopping for the perfect clothes, dorm items and saying goodbye to her many high school friends many of which she had been with since first grade. It was an exciting time for her in anticipation of being on her own and she was happy at the thought of not having her mother around asking her to do things. My children tend to tell me I bug them too much by telling them to do chores around the house. My response has always been, "What is the point of having kids if they don't do things for you?"

I was planning my first trip to Houston since January. I was actually looking forward to a three-day escape even though it was work. After twenty years of marriage, I finally figured it out…..it is fun to make money, so I can have someone else clean my house and when I travel I can order room service. I considered myself fortunate to be given such a wonderful opportunity of holding a very sought after position that required travel to exciting destinations. I often ask myself, "Does life get any better than this?"

I have always enjoyed the open road travel. It grants me the freedom to stop at the many roadside antique shops, be the commander of the remote control, and experience a bubble bath without anyone calling my name. Traveling allowed me to have some "me" time and embrace the quiet. I love leaving my house with an empty car and coming back with my newfound treasures. My favorite finds are antique Bibles, old leather bound books, guest towels and vintage purses. I find it fascinating to view a Bible containing a stranger's personal information along with personal hand-written notes, often marking their favorite scriptures. I find it so interesting to imagine other people's lives in another place and time and my vintage collection take me on a journey in my mind. I pretend to know and feel someone's emotions while reading a scripture verse.

My work trip to Houston was all planned and I was ready to head out, but not before an early appointment with yet another doctor. After multiple test it was that my determined that my thyroid medication was not the cause of my excruciating headaches. So it was off to the sinus specialist before another departure to the open road.

Immediately upon entering the room Dr. Gerald Grey directly informed me of his prognosis. The culprit was several polyps in my right sinus cavity. He said they would need to be removed as soon as possible. I was speechless, as I was saying to myself - here we go again! I explained that I had undergone two surgeries in the last five months and didn't feel like I could endure another. The doctor calmly and patiently explained that to me that he was not giving me the option of surgery, but the option of when I wanted it to occur. I immediately felt that overwhelming sensation returning; the same sensation that consumed me right before my cancer surgery. My first thoughts, "How is Doug going to respond to me having another surgery? How and why is this happening again?" I had already missed so much work that the thought of asking for more time off put me in a complete panic. I couldn't tell anyone that I was having another surgery because it was just too embarrassing. When did I become so high maintenance? Once again I entered "It's Business" mode and asked the doctor for his first available date. I decided that if it had to be done then it was going to be done right away. The less said the better and taking time off in the summer was far less noticeable than in the fall. I convinced myself of this and it made me feel better.

The surgery date was set for the following week, and when I returned to the car I immediately called Doug to give him the surprising news. As I headed down the highway towards Houston, I could not hold back the tears. I was so tired of all the health drama. I felt so depressed. Once again, Interstate 45 was again for me a long and lonely journey. Another health issue presents itself within six months of my memorable road trip to the energy city. The old feelings from that trip six months prior flooded my soul. My heart was heavy, and once again I felt the stress and pressure of another looming surgery.

This time my drive to the most metropolitan city of Texas did not include any random, therapeutic stops. I was pressed for time with several afternoon appointments, and having already experienced this journey literally and figuratively caused me to press on. I knew staying busy with work was the best thing I could do for my mental health and myself. Idle time would send my mind in a bad direction and strengthen my stress and fear.

My work day was a success and I was pleasantly surprised to finish early, around 4 o'clock on a splendid, sunny day. I was not quite sure what to do next; I found myself just driving around looking for something to do, seeking something that I desperately needed, but having no idea what it was. I wasn't comfortable sitting in an establishment by myself sipping a glass of wine, so I searched for a local spa to relieve my mind and body. I have always said, "When stressed go get a beauty treatment." I knew this was a better strategy than drinking. As I looked up, I saw a captivating phrase advertising "sugar waxing." Of course, I became immediately intrigued.

The cars in the shopping center parking lot were upscale. My inquisitive nature had firmly kicked in. I approached the establishment and to my surprise the front door was locked so I rang the bell, and immediately heard a click and the door unlock.

As I entered the reception area I was politely greeted by an attractive, sharply dressed lady who asked me how she could be of assistance. The two ladies sitting in the waiting area resembled a couple of my friends and we made brief eye contact and then looked away. I hesitantly asked the woman behind the counter, "What exactly do you all do?" The "sugar waxing" billboard ad motivated my curiosity. I was not really sure what I was about to sign up for; I was just going with the moment. I felt like I was an undercover police officer setting up a sting operation. The woman kindly replied, "What do you think we do?" I paused as my mind scrambled for a logical answer and responded, "You do Brazilian waxes?" All three women laughed out loud as I suddenly felt out of place and somewhat intimidated. My curiosity about the waxing was at full throttle. If I was ever going to have the nerve to do that, this was the time. I felt so uneasy and out of sorts over my impending surgery that doing something typically outside my comfort zone seemed right. Maybe having my hair ripped out of my skin down there would ease my stress. My heart was telling me to do something unconventional while my head was telling me that I'm crazy. Besides if it did not relieve my anxiety, I'm sure the pain would temporarily make me forget about my health issues.

The lady promptly responded, "Yes we do. Would you like one?" I gasped for a breath and turned to one of the ladies and asked, "Do you get one?" She confidently replied "Yes, of course." I turned to the other woman and nodded my head for a response to the very personal question. She nodded back and said, "Absolutely!" I was a bit confused. Where had I been? I didn't even know this procedure existed until just a few years ago. But then again, thanks to Bill Clinton and Monica Lewinsky there was another trend going on in this country too.

My surprise and uncertainty turned into a bold, defiant confidence as I firmly planted my feet and replied, "Yes, I want one!" The receptionist grinned with approval, instructed me to take some over-the-counter medicine and come back in one hour. She was clearly amused by our interchange, but I couldn't tell if she was laughing with me or at me. I suspect she thought I wouldn't be back, but I was determined to explore the unknown. I went out to the car and took the pain reliever. Just then I decided to bring out the heavy artillery. This moment certainly qualified. In case of an emergency I had a reserve stash of prescription pain medicine left over from the previous surgery. It was as good a time as any. I popped one and then thought, "Maybe should go for two."

I now had an hour to kill with a soon-to-be very relaxed mind and body so I did some window shopping. I wasn't sure if I would keep the appointment, but I made a conscious decision not to call anyone for their opinion, including Doug. Of course, I knew I could change my mind within the hour, but I was leaning towards going for it.

At five o'clock straight up I rang the bell and entered the store for the moment of truth. Once again the lady laughed and confirmed my suspicion that she didn't think I was going to show. She told me she rarely takes walk-ins but she knew I was a first timer and in her words "So Darn Funny" that she couldn't resist encouraging me. She worked late to accommodate my request and when I thanked her she chuckled and said, "Let's see if you thank me when it's finished." As I jumped onto the table I was in a full sweat. I thought I must be losing my mind or having an out of body experience. Either way, it occurred to me that I could be in serious trouble once this was done and it was time to return home.

The first pull was the most painful thing I had ever experienced. The ripping off of my hair from the roots had me screaming expletives at the top of my lungs. My mouth sounded like twelve sailors lost at sea. Needless to say, my mother would not have approved of my potty mouth. I had to take a deep breath and regroup my thoughts to prepare for another attack. I knew I couldn't remain "as is" for if I was in a wreck on the way home and the paramedics had to cut off my clothes, they would assume I had been attacked by a group of Apache Indians.

The next hour was one of the worst of my life. I must admit my spontaneous spa treatment accomplished my goal of doing something outside the box to relieve the anxiety of my upcoming surgery. In that sixty minutes I forgot all about surgery and frankly, I really didn't care. I took my sore, bruised and bleeding body back to the hotel and remained on pain relievers for the next few days.

With my surgery just days away I prayed my hospital gown would not fly open and reveal my new twisted secret!

CHAPTER 8
Education Creates Freedom and Enables Power

IT SEEMED SO MUCH TIME had flown by in such a short period, and the previous six months often masqueraded as two years. I couldn't believe all the crazy things I had experienced and still, the constant nag of having cancer in my body was tugging on me every day. The fear of the unknown plagued me. Perhaps my biggest challenge was the lack of control I had over my life and body. I had spent years perfecting the art of control. My life was all about it. Only to discover I really never had it nor will I ever. I just wanted to know if all the bad cells were gone. If not, I wanted to know what would be required of me to demand a cancer free body. Little did I know what was in store for me around the corner? Other than the terror of cancer, I could not think of anything worse than what I was about to face.

I can vividly remember that early summer morning. I was working in my office, when my boss quietly summoned me to his office. I was eager to hear an update on the progress of the internal office restructuring and find out where I would be working after the changes were implemented. I entered Dr. Stanwick's office, of whom I had fondly thought of, sort of a father figure. He asked me to shut the door and take a seat. In a kind voice he started the conversation with "we have a problem." I suddenly wilted inside, as I knew what he was about to say. I answered, "I know what it is. Someone in our department has discovered I do not have my degree." He had a serious and firm look on his face and said, "Yes, and it's a real problem." For a brief moment, I was eight-years-old again with the same feelings as an elementary school child. The formal education issue was once again rearing its ugly head as it was once again piercing my soul. This had really become a thorn in my side. My failure to complete my college education now had immeasurable consequences to my family and me. My other colleagues were raising the issue and the office gossip was at full capacity. He gave me the option to travel three weeks a month or return to the classroom and complete my education. It was not just about pay scale and tuition benefits, but about the example I was setting for my children. My non-degree status had been previously spoken by others, but honestly, I didn't have much need for a college degree up to this point. However, if this issue was going to hinder my ability to succeed as an employee at my current place of business I owed it to myself and my family to acknowledge what had become the large elephant in the room. I sat still for a brief moment before jumping to my feet. Without hesitation I blurted out, "Then I will go back to school!"

After I spoke the words out loud it dawned on me I was in way over my head. What did I just commit to? How am I going to pull this off? Let's see; married, three kids, working full time, cancer, maybe more surgery, three surgeries this year, moved twice, a new house, child starting college, child in high school, child in 5th grade, child starting sorority rush, child with knee injury who is unable to play sports and now I am committing to going back to school? All these questions raced through my brain at warp speed. I had an entire conversation with a mental panic attack with myself in just seconds. The most unusual feeling came over me. It was as if time was frozen and my mind zoomed into focus on this one vision. In that moment I could truly see how much I had learned from my daughter, Bailey, from a race she ran seven years prior. I had no idea at the time that a middle school track meet would foster a defining moment in my life years later. In regards to my education, my path mirrored Bailey's running of the hurdles. I had fallen down, but was given the opportunity to finish the race even though it was twenty years later. What an amazing gift I had been given. It is strange how life-changing moments are etched into our minds and memories. When these moments occur we have no warning signs that drop down to tell us "pay attention; life changing moment ahead." We only realize later that what we experienced has been stamped into our hearts and heads forever. I remember being confused by it at the time, but the imagery was dramatic:

In my mind I could see Bailey running on the track with the crowd screaming and cheering her on. With each stride and the perfect timing of each footstep, she leaped through the air gracefully gliding over each wooden obstacle. One by one, she approached each hurdle and with each stride as she calculated her rhythm with great anticipation. Then suddenly out of nowhere, an untied shoestring became her enemy. She felt an immediate unbalance with her body weight and she threw her arms out in front of herself to catch her falling body. As she came crashing down, her legs hit the white wooden stand and her body weight landed on her right arm. She fell to the hard ground at full speed as if the earth was moving toward her at an uncontrollable pace. Ignoring the screams in the crowd, she immediately stood to her feet and slowly regained the familiar course. With tears flowing down her cheeks, a broken dangling arm, blood dripping down her legs and embarrassment from the fall she set her eyes on the finish line. As she placed each step in front of the other she felt immense pain, but she focused her eyes on completing the race. Bailey encountered a difficult situation and with determination she finished the race!

Getting a degree is something I have always wanted to do, so I thought to myself, "How many people do I know who get a second chance?" I tried to pull myself together and refocus on the conversation with my superior. Dr. Stanwick began to detail the university's policy and procedure for an employee going back to school. According to him I was eligible to receive six hours of tuition per semester ($667 per hour) and with my superior's approval I could take three of those hours during work time. He explained that as long as I continued to work and perform to my ability, I would be able to continue my education. I must admit I was thrilled at the opportunity and felt it would be a wonderful example to set for my children.

I left the Dr. Stanwick's office scared, excited, and extremely grateful for my new opportunity. I was feeling and believing the words that I often say to my children: "Education creates freedom and enables power!" I was going to receive that freedom and soon earn the power.

CHAPTER 9
There Goes my Baby

THE RECOVERY FROM MY THIRD surgery for my sinuses was longer than expected, but the results were definitely worth it. A wise man once said: "nothing in life is ever easy." My life had become a testament to this statement.

Summer was gaining momentum and the university campus was preparing for the return of students for the fall semester. I was excited that Bailey was moving into her new college room, even if her dormitory room was right across the street from my office. She worried that I might invade her space, but I decided to give her the license to leave, and I resigned myself that I would respect her freedom. The truth is she needed to leave. It was becoming more and more apparent that our close relationship was being challenged everyday with us in the house together. Another wise man once said: "All good things must come to an end." It was time for my daughter to leave the house.

Doug and I always had encouraged our children to leave town for a college for at least one year. We both did that (me to Oxford, Mississippi and Doug to Lexington, Virginia) primarily because we were independent people and we tried to instill that in our children. I changed my mind after becoming sick and Doug was on board as well. Typically I was firm in my decisions, especially important decisions pertaining to family. One life-changing experience caused me to rethink the "independence" strategy. To be perfectly honest there was some selfishness here, but after Doug and I discussed it we were firmly on the same page, and to our surprise, Bailey enthusiastically embraced the decision to attend college in Fort Worth.

I was really relieved to have Bailey on campus. I knew if I became sick again I would need her close, even if we had never discussed it. I knew she was thinking the same thing. I had come face to face with the reality of how our time on this earth is limited. This realization caused me to desire easy access to my children. Having Bailey physically close to me gave me comfort and peace of mind. Some may view this as selfish and twisted thinking, but at least I wasn't in denial; I made my intentions and motivations clear and thanked God for my family and embraced them.

College move-in day was a grand production for all the families except ours. Doug and I never bought into many of the normal school processes that many of the other parents turned into huge events. Bailey insisted that she move herself, and demanded as little assistance as possible from her parents, a clear indication that the "independence" thing had sunk in. She was ready to leave, but moving across the street from her mother's work place did not seem like a good thing to her. She resented having to share a campus with her mom even though I was there first. She started to doubt her college choice because she did not want to run in to me on campus, much less hear about me taking classes. Walking to class was difficult for me. I found myself hiding behind my sunglasses and zoning out to music on my shuffle. I felt like an outcast in my own neighborhood. Bailey and her friends didn't want to see me in the "their" environment and would rarely speak to me in public when I encountered them on campus. Not only was I the oldest person in their class, but also I had to wear my "cheaters" aka reading glasses to read anything. At this time in my life I had very low self-esteem; however, my lack of success in the past demanded that I pay a price for my future success. I had to complete this "degree thing" in order to keep my job, continue my medical benefits, and provide tuition benefits for my children. Certainly these were motivating factors, but setting a good example for my children became my biggest inspiration and presented a huge challenge. I had preached to my kids daily that "Education Creates Freedom and Enables Power." This statement compelled me, to lead by example, and I was not going to let Bailey's embarrassment of my presence on campus comprise my resolve.

Sororities had a strong presence on campus and Bailey was excited to start her sorority recruitment. I tried to keep my secret wishes for her to myself, but again our closeness caused her to know my wishes without articulating them. I remember the first day of the process quite vividly. I was becoming anxious about the first round of the sorority selection process when a phone call interrupted my fretfulness.

On the other end of the phone was a nurse who kindly stated: "It is time for your six-month scan." This was the scan I had waited for since my surgery and I was anxious about. This was the scan that was supposed to make me more of a patient woman. Yes, scan time was finally here and I immediately thought "Not now!" My daughter was in college and starting sorority recruitment. The timing was wrong.

I listened carefully to the nurse on the phone of what would be required of me during this weeklong medical procedure. The scan consisted of two shots in both hips over the first two consecutive days, followed by the administration of a nuclear medicine pill in the hospital before entering a closed MRI tunnel on the last day of the week. Once the scan started, I would be confined to a small space for about an hour. I reached into my "mantra" bag and pulled out my two favorite reminders: break it down into "Baby Steps" and "Take One Day at a Time." Irrational and uncontrollable thinking insisted I take the necessary actions to regain my composure. "Mind over matter" was required in that fearful moment. I suddenly entered a peaceful state and smiled. I immediately felt God's hand with me as he knew I was going into that tunnel alone and his protection would be with me the entire time. Once again I could feel His hand in my life and I was confident of His perfect timing. Here I was stressing out about sorority recruitment and the bigger stress I was facing was if my cancer was gone. Sometimes I just get so embarrassed in front of myself for my ridiculous thinking.

I got to my feet, walked around my desk and down the hall toward one of my colleagues. I went from tears to laughter as I shared with her the craziness of my life. Within minutes, I was feeling so blessed. I was thankful for Bailey's opportunity to be part of the recruitment process instead of viewing her as a "recruitment" victim, she I saw her as a "recruitment" participator.

It was a time to embrace and enjoy the opportunity to participate in everything we do...

God's timing really is perfect and I was being
reminded of this day after day!

CHAPTER 10
Too Much Coffee

THE SCAN REVEALED THE SURGERY and the radiation treatment was successful. Bailey had completed the recruitment process and things were looking up for our family. I was enjoying my classes much more than I ever expected. Learning as an adult was exhilarating. I am not sure where I was the first four years of college, but now at the age of 44 my mind and body had finally made it to the classroom!

The reconstruction of the internal office had taken place with including a new boss and department. I was sad not to have Susan Christy and Dr. Stanwick as my superiors, but excited for the new opportunity. The fall semester flew by and with the start of a new year would bring another cancer scan as well as my yearly job appraisal.

Before tackling the cancer scan I was looking forward to my annual job evaluation. I had participated in one previously and found it to be an excellent learning experience. The process had proved to be a useful tool for communication and for obtaining my future goals and objectives. Communication had become one of my strengths. The yearly job evaluation mapped my employer's expectations while leading to higher production and performance.

I had been under the direction of a new supervisor, Jackson Hyde, for two months. Jackson, an ex- letterman, was also a popular sports recruiter who covered most of the university's major sporting events. He was fairly known in the athletic community and very familiar to the university's fans, but unknown to me.

As I entered his office for the evaluation, he immediately took charge, opening the conversation with a surprising statement, "I know you have had cancer and I know that it has affected your performance, but I want you to know under my supervision your numbers will improve." At first, I didn't know how to take the audacious remark, and the aggressive tone of his voice put me in shock. I felt my posture straightening as I prepared to defend myself and my job performance. I could feel a heat rising in my body. I felt like a mother protecting her child, but in this case, I was protecting myself. He made me feel as if having cancer was a character flaw and that it was something under my control. At that very moment I realized I must take a stand for myself and for other cancer survivors who may be discriminated against because of their disease. What made matters worse was his statement was not true. In fact, it was quite the opposite. My evaluation from the previous year was positive, accurate and motivating:

Name: Nancy Woodson
Title: Officer
Length in position: 11 months
Evaluation:

Battling cancer has not slowed her down and she remains focused on achieving her primary goals for the year. Her spirit is unbreakable and sheer determination drives her to success.......

Jackson's two-month assessment of my performance was incorrect. According to him I had not worked to my full potential, but under his direction I would become a more productive worker. Jackson was relatively new in his position having previously managed a small team in the used car business. Perhaps he felt he must assert himself in an attempt to impress his new boss? His words made my skin crawl and I felt sick inside. I had conducted my work in a professional manner, and I was proud of my progress and success. I had reached my production goals despite through any medical absences or by my disease. I had achieved success for my team and for myself.

Once I had gathered myself I responded, to his proclamation, "Excuse me? Cancer did not slow me down and I resent your statement. I have worked very hard and yes, I have cancer, but that has not limited my production and my work. I don't think you are qualified to make that judgment because you were not here during my illness." I could not believe the words flowed from my mouth. My heart became full of anger and disbelief. I was sitting in front of a man who was criticizing me for having cancer, while raising a family, working full time, and going to school. I was stunned.

For the second time, I could feel others saw me has having the "big C." It was the strangest, most unsettling feeling. If anything my illness had motivated me to work harder and become a better person. No evidence to the contrary my positive approach was working. I wasn't looking for excuses; it spurred me on to achieve more. I was not going to take the easy way out, not now. I was committed to my family, my job and continuing my education. Although the university had demanded I get a degree, I felt it was a privilege to receive a second chance to complete my higher education. People often asked me why I was loading so much on my plate. I always gave the same response: "Because I can and because I have been given the opportunity." With that opportunity I would strive for my personal best with the 3 D's: Dedication, Drive and Determination.

My mind flashed back to my admissions essay and I felt like Dorothy going down the yellow brick road. I had the sensation that I was approaching another detour in the road and my journey was starting to become more difficult. So many thoughts and feelings entered my head within those minutes. How many people have been given a second chance? I realized I was physically, emotionally and now financially contributing to my family. I loved being able to provide for my children's education. It was a wonderful feeling and added to my self-esteem.

I quickly decided to swallow my pride and just let his demeaning remarks go. This was the path of least resistance. He offered to follow up with specific goals for my job description, along with a list of potential donors. The meeting ended with a "to do" list for us both.

The weekly staff meeting was a standard requirement for our team. Each week we would discuss each person's job responsibilities as well as the team's goals for the days ahead.

When out of the blue a weekly staff meeting took on an unusual turn of events. The meeting started at a normal pace, when suddenly Jackson displayed signs of what an innocent by stander could view as a high level of testosterone. The volume of his voice elevated as he pounded his hand on the desk several times during the discussion. Apparently, Jackson had an overdose of caffeine. His behavior was completely erratic. His inappropriate language intensified as he used the word "dick" four times, derogatorily referring to other staff members.

The mood of the meeting became tense and the three middle-aged staff women at his desk were uncomfortable to say the least. I was not sure how to respond to this bizarre behavior, I kiddingly asked him, "How much coffee have you had this morning?" The teasing comment seemed to break the tension a little in an effort to lighten the moment. The meeting ended shortly thereafter.

As the three older ladies left his office, we were all in shock over his unprofessional behavior. One of them said, "My husband would be so mad if he knew he was talking to us like that." We all shook our heads in disgust as we all returned to our desk.

Jackson never apologized for his outburst combined with his disrespectful language to our team. His multiple outbursts increased over time and it was becoming more and more obvious to our team of the changing dynamics to the group.

Another year had come and gone and what a twelve months it had been. In some ways, the twelve months felt like a few weeks with everyone's busy schedules. I was approaching my one-year cancer anniversary, anxiously waiting for a clear scan. I had so many emotions and thoughts racing through my heart and head. What if the cancer was still growing in my body? What if I need more surgery? How was I going to balance my family, work and school with another setback? Cancer plays such a mind trip with your thoughts. The very word causes fear and anxiety, but the uncertainty and waiting was something I was not prepared for. At the end of the day, there are no guarantees in life except our salvation, death, and taxes! Salvation makes me smile, death motivates me to live each day to its fullest and taxes make me feel broke.

In honor of my cancer free, one-year anniversary I decided to treat myself to a full body physical examination at the Cooper Clinic in Dallas. I arranged for a full day of various tests with multiple body scans, including a detailed evaluation of my health status. I passed the physical with flying colors with one exception multiple gallstones. The examination would be my reward to myself after receiving a clean report as well as the craziest pair of embroidery cowboy boots.

My friends, on the other hand, had all decided to mark my one-year cancer free anniversary with a group celebration. A surprise party with multiple friends was just another reminder of the many people in my life who supported me during my illness. Doug surprised me as well by hiring the family singing group, the McCampbells. This was the same group that inspired me one year earlier when I was facing my thyroid surgery. The five-member group entertained the guest with the many beautiful gospel hymns. My friends were so overwhelmed with the singing family's gift of praise that after several encores the McCampbells joined our party as dinner guests. The night was amazing and my new gospel friends were a reminder to me of God's grace and love. Through this difficult time in my life, I was exposed to another culture as well as another way to worship. Each person felt a connection to this gifted family and everyone in the room could feel their love.

Life continued to move at a rapid pace with family, work and school. My fear of the returning cancer weighed heavy on my mind, and regularly I think the fear was more debilitating than the disease. The regular scheduled doctor appointments with scans became part of my life. I never realized the maintenance of cancer with regular scans and blood work, not to mention the financial obligations.

CHAPTER 11
Nancy Ann

THE SUMMER WAS MOVING ALONG at a rapid pace. The Texas heat lingered like a long-winded friend, something I might enjoy while relaxing by the pool, but who soon became a nuisance.

My workload was increasing as I was continuing my academic plan. I quickly discovered that my brain no longer operated at the capacity it once had. My mind often drifted to my daily tasks, away from the focus I needed to excel academically. I had always desired to get my degree, but now that I was basically being required to do so, I made the decision that just getting the hours to graduate was not enough. I had to do so by performing at a high level, therefore, each grade for each class was a big deal to me. I had to breakdown each and every day-to-day obligation, and all my responsibilities into "Baby Steps." I had to constantly remind myself to "Take One Day at a Time." Maturity had after all taught me everything would all still be there at the end of the day. If by chance someone took away the items on my-to-do list, I would welcome the help.

My son Jay was preparing for his senior year. His daily workouts marked the start of the approaching football season. The girls were enjoying their time with their friends, delighting in spontaneous activities and poolside parties. Doug was pulling long workdays but graciously offered to share in the many family responsibilities. The good news for me is I married a man who enjoys cooking, which came in handy often.

Our family was preparing to drive to San Antonio for my niece's wedding. She is the oldest of twenty-four grandchildren and the first to get married. The logistics of getting our family of five to the Alamo City with the many different schedules were becoming quite a challenge. After much discussion, we determined taking two cars was the best plan of action. The "girls" left early to share an adventure… shopping at the outlet malls and antique stores along the way.

It was such a treat to see my brothers, sisters, aunts, uncles, and many nieces and nephews. Our family had grown quite large boasting eight children, six in law children and twenty-four grandchildren. My parents were thrilled to have their entire family together, however, my oldest sister, Terry, did not make trip because she was not feeling well.

Terry was the second of the eight children, and she was starting to distance herself from our family. Her communication with all of us had become limited conversations over the phone and through emails. At this time I suspected she was abusively drinking, but each time I broached the subject she would deny it, but I knew I was right. Over time she was attending fewer and fewer family functions and would rarely leave her home. We were only twenty minutes travel time apart from door to door, but with my busy schedule personal visits were a challenge. We spoke on the phone every day and our relationship was strong. Terry loved to cook and always offered to prepare meals for my family during the week and every holiday. I regularly requested for our families to be together for Thanksgiving, Christmas and birthdays, but she consistently declined each and every time.

The first day in San Antonio was a wonderful family adventure. Three of my sisters hosted a bridesmaid lunch, and later we all walked along the famous river walk. The day turned out to be perfect. The group decided to take a riverboat ride in the late afternoon due to the beautiful summer conditions. The early evening was delightful and we all enjoyed the special time with the many girls in our family was a real treat.

As we entered the barge called the "river boat" and settled in for the sightseeing ride, I casually checked all emails on my PDA. I had no idea how monumental the message I was about to receive would ultimately be. As I scrolled down through my inbox, I came across an email from my boss, Jackson Hyde. As I began to read his message, a panic attack came upon me and stole the pleasantness of my afternoon almost instantly. Here is a copy of the email:

(sic)
From: Jackson, Hyde
Date: Thu, 15 Jun 2006
To:"Woodson, Nancy"
Subject: Planning Items NW

When you return from your trip, we need to sit down and discuss your plans for the fall semester as far as classes go.
We are going to be very busy and I am planning a heavy schedule for you - Don't plan on any daytime classes on your schedule.
Just a "heads-up" for you. We'll talk when you get back.
Jackson

I can remember that day vividly. At the time I had no idea of the conflict and chaos that was about to ensue. Being allowed to take three hours of school during the day was instrumental to my academic success. It was physically and emotionally impossible for me to care for my family, work a forty-hour work week, take six hours at night and attend sixty work events a year. Jackson's increasing demands would compromise my education and complicate my life. The statement in his email confused me. Eleven months prior I was assured by the university, I would be able to continue my education provided I maintain all work demands with strong job appraisal. Under the university's policy, I qualified for six hours a semester in free tuition. Three of those hours were to be taken during the forty-hour workweek. All of a sudden, out of the blue, I was informed without any warning that the opportunity was off the table and I was no longer eligible for the benefit. I took a deep breath and quickly responded to his email:

From: Woodson, Nancy
Sent: Thu 6/15/2006
To: Jackson, Hyde
Subject: Re: Planning Items

I guess we need to discuss this because when I was told I given this position, taking day classes was part of the deal.

Jackson's response:

(sic)
From: Jackson, Hyde
Date: Thu, 15 Jun 2006
To:"Woodson, Nancy"
Subject: RE: Planning Items

We'll visit. I know I was not involved in any such discussions and, because of the obvious conflicts with your job during the day, it needs to be addressed.

I fully support what you taking classes and would like to understand more about your degree plan, but I'm also concerned that we get the work of Donor Club done first. That needs to be the priority of everyone on the staff.

Jackson

The remaining vacation was preoccupied with the stress of returning to work and having to fight upper management. I reminded myself to "Take One Day at a Time" and enjoy the 3f's....forced family fun! The five Woodsons (in two cars) returned to Fort Worth on Sunday and I was anxious to call Terry to share the fun details of the weekend. There were so many family stories to discuss, but my real focus was on Jackson's threat that I may not be allowed to continue my academic game plan. I immediately shared Jackson's email with Terry and asked her how I should handle the situation.

I can remember her exact words: "I am so proud of you Nancy Ann!" She knew I had always hated my name, but through humor, we both found laughter and her compliment briefly relieved my stress. It was said in a loving moment and those few words comforted me and gave me strength.

Why didn't I like my name? I don't know why, but I never did. Perhaps it was because I spent my first three days nameless in a hospital crib. Maybe it was because the name Nancy always reminded me of the full figured, black-headed cartoon character from the newspaper. Whatever the reason, I had developed a dislike for "Nancy Ann." For the first time, I heard my name in a different way. I liked the person she was talking about, I admired her work ethic and I wanted to be her. I found myself smiling and for a few seconds, my mind actually drifted away from school and work. It was a special moment...one of those life-changing things...I finally liked my name!

CHAPTER 12
This was not in the Brochure

THE NEXT MORNING, I RELUCTANTLY entered Jackson's office on that early Monday morning to discuss the email that disrupted my family retreat, as I wanted to face the issue head on and get it resolved promptly. Not knowing where he was coming from made me terribly uncomfortable. Were his intentions sincere because it was true that he was not involved in the discussions last year or were they insincere in an effort to control my schedule?

As I sat down at his desk, he immediately informed me that he was not going to allow me to take any classes on "his" time. His terse and matter-of-fact words stopped me dead in my tracks. I had a sensation that time was standing still, and I didn't know how I should respond.

"I'm sorry?" I replied. "That was not the deal the university offered me during the reorganization from my prior position." I started to recount the details of the arrangement to him only to be rudely interrupted, "Don't Care," he said. "Your previous supervisor is not your boss now, I am." He raised his voice to make the point that this was his decision and the past promises made months earlier would not be honored. He went on to say my previous supervisor was a "has been" on this campus and he had the support of the Vice Chancellor and one of the university's "top alumni." He was convinced that this was his call and the powers to be had granted him "free" reign and he was determined to make sure I wouldn't question it. It was bewildering and disappointing that my new superior openly criticized the man who hired me. Dr. Stanwick had been with the school for over fifteen years and was respected on the campus and in our community. In short, he was a fine, honest man.

The disrespectful comment and the aggressiveness of his mean spirited words left me speechless, which is a rare occurrence. In hind sight, I was convinced the unsettling conversation actually had little to do about me and more about Jackson's power and ego. At that moment after gathering my thoughts, I felt compelled to fight for my education and my rights based on the previously agreed commitments. I also felt an intense obligation to defend my previous mentor.

Jackson continued the conversation with the question: "Just how much longer do you have until you graduate?" I calmly responded, "I'm not sure, but I will be meeting with my advisor every semester to track my progress." He then asked me if something was going on with my health because if there was he stated, he wanted me to tell him and not have to hear it from the other girls in the office. The conversation remained tense. Jackson suggested he would arrange a meeting for me to meet with one of his "advisors." In an arrogant manner, he dictated that he would attend the meeting to find out how long it would take to complete my degree. He thought his advisor would be able to suggest some "creative" ideas on how to speed up the process. I was skeptical and unsure as to why he found it necessary to attend a confidential meeting pertaining solely to my academic career.

I was floored with his presumptuous involvement in my personal business. At this time I knew little about any schools' privacy policy relative to academics, but I did know that his approach and demands felt inappropriate and wrong. I resisted the urge to debate this further and thanked him for his assistance. I did not mention in closing I would not be comfortable with him viewing my transcript and coming to the meeting. After all, I'm the girl who hid her transcript in her underwear drawer in shame for over twenty years. As I stood up to leave his office he forcefully responded, "It's my call and I will attend the meeting."

I felt a panic attack coming on. I have always been insecure and apologetic about my "degree" issue and revisiting the topic with my new, strict supervisor made me very uneasy and stressed. I timidly expressed how he must have felt like he had won the "booby" prize by inheriting me in an attempt to interject humor, but he didn't appreciate the light hearted comment. He got the sick girl who didn't have her degree and he viewed me and my situation as a burdensome problem that he was determined to solve. Then, I told him that I did not want him to be present in my academic counseling. I quickly changed the subject and abruptly left his office, feeling embarrassed and belittled by the entire ordeal. Nevertheless, he was my boss, so I knew I must address this appropriately, and I wanted to believe he had my best interest at heart, but I was starting to doubt his intentions.

It's difficult to describe what I was feeling at the end of that conversation. I had never experienced such treatment in the working world. It was as if I had no rights and little control over my personal business. Certainly my academic information was not going to be made a public record. I knew I had a right to privacy, but deep down I wondered if I was stirring up the hornet's nest by protesting. It seemed like I was being "bullied," but I couldn't quite get my mind around what was really going on. I was determined to fight for my previously approved daytime hours to attend class. I had already made a commitment and had time invested in study and activities away from my family. That night I was overwhelmed with stress and cried a couple of times while thinking about the day's meeting. My family felt my pain as I recited the scene over and over. I couldn't get it out of my mind. Not only had this man raised his voice and demeaned me, but he had also infringed upon my academic personal privacy.

The next day I visited my academic advisor, Caroline Wilson to ask her if she would attend the upcoming meeting with the new academic advisor, Mark Hamilton. She promptly agreed and raised my comfort level immensely. She refrained from commenting on Jackson's directives but her disapproval of his aggressive action was evident in her facial expressions.

As the next few days passed I felt a deep sadness inside. I was unsure of what to do and even wondered if there was anything I could do, not just about the class time, but also about the harassment, inappropriate language, and the multiple outburst that probably infringed upon my credibility. Out of the blue, it dawned on me that I could contact his superior to reveal his approach and find out if he had the authority that he claimed. I knew this would be risky, but I felt confident that I could defend my work production and academic plan. I decided to plead my case for taking the three hours of class during the day, together with a request that something be done to reign in Jackson's aggressive behavior.

I immediately sent an email to his boss, Walter Phillips requesting an intervention to this stressful situation.

From: Woodson, Nancy
Sent: Tuesday, June 20, 2006
To: Phillips, Walter
Subject: Tuesday

Walter,
Can I please meet with you today? I am open anytime.
Thanks,
Nancy

He responded immediately:

From: Phillips, Walter
Sent: Tuesday, June 20, 2006
To: Woodson, Nancy
Subject: RE: Tuesday
Nancy:
How about 10 AM? I need to leave for a meeting by 11.
Walter

From: Woodson, Nancy
Sent: Tuesday, June 20, 2006
To: Phillips, Walter
Subject: RE: Tuesday
Perfect – see you then

Jackson had left that morning for a business trip so leaving my office for my meeting with his superior Walter was less stressful as no one thought anything of me leaving the office to meet with him across campus. As I entered Walter's office I was somewhat surprised that I was actually asking for his assistance with Jackson. I was reluctant to share my appointment with Walter with anyone, even Doug. My fear was that I would be discouraged from making such an aggressive move. I was confident in my decision even though I knew there could be negative repercussions. I made the choice to stand up for myself, the quality of my work and my academic plan. I had kept my part of the bargain by keeping my production up and I expected my employer to keep their part by allowing me to take 3 hours of class during the work day.

I opened the meeting with Walter by stating that I was present on my own behalf only and was not speaking for anyone else in the office. I assured Walter that I had not confided in any other staff members as these issues were only affecting me. I laid out the following issues:

1.) During my interview for this new position I was told that I would be required to attend a few required events. Jackson demanded I attend the entire 60 events throughout the year. Keep in mind these were in addition to the 40 hour work week.

2.) It was previously agreed that I could take three hour of classes during the day so long as my work did not suffer. My production was as good as ever, but Jackson made it clear that I would not be allowed to attend classes on "his" time.

3.) Jackson's behavior toward me was inappropriate and included yelling, vulgar language, and disrespect.

I also explained to Walter that Jackson had never given me any type of goals, a list of prospects or a job description with specific tasks or direction for my position. I let him know that I had asked Jackson several times to contact donor relations for my donor assignments. He never responded to my request in this regard. I offered Walter a detailed list of new gifts I had solicited and received, many of whom had no connection to the university as I was instrumental in securing donations from them.

Walter listened attentively and was very gracious during our hour-long conversation. He told me that he would speak to Jackson regarding my contentions, and what I considered to be the overstepping of his authority regarding my career and education. I was nervous about the pending conversation that was to take place, but I was confident that my action was the right one and was truly appreciative of Walter's assistance on what I considered very serious issues. Walter said he would contact me with the details of their conversation and would advise me of any progress; however, I never received any type of follow up from our meeting which caused me great concern. I did receive a long distance call from Jackson, but he remained firm regarding his attendance of the upcoming academic meeting. I knew then it was time to take another approach and seek to the next level of help with this situation.

Later that day I sent Jackson the following email:

From: Woodson, Nancy
Sent: Tuesday, June 20, 2006
To: Hyde, Jackson
Cc: Phillips, Walter
Subject: '07 request

Jackson,

I wanted you to be aware that I spoke with Walter about our conversation yesterday along with many other things. I am feeling quite frustrated with the fact that when I was hired I was told I can continue my education and taking three hours during the day was acceptable.

As you requested, I am preparing my plan for FY 07. To do this, I am requesting from you the exact number of events I should attend for the year and would appreciate a specific job description for my position and a projected goal (both dollars to be raised and the number of calls on donors) for FY '07. I spoke with research today and my prospects have never been transferred to me and she has requested for me to fill out the appropriate paper work to complete the process, so my numbers will reflect my effort.

Thank you.
Nancy Woodson

Nancy Woodson
Donor Club

I was upset and confused about my rights as a student and an employee so the following day I called Stephanie Brown at Human Resources and requested an informal visit to discuss my situation and get another perspective. I explained to her that I was not really sure if I had a legitimate reason to be in her office. With little experience in business I was unaware of what it meant to see the Human Resources Director. I further explained my belief that this man was bullying me in an inappropriate way. I described how I felt my education was in jeopardy and that it was a very sensitive issue for me. I told her I was not willing to be judged or humiliated over my previous mistakes concerning my academic past. I was trying to set an example of the importance of an education for my children.

Stephanie interrupted by raising her hand in the air and said "Stop."

Without any hesitation she stated: "Jackson has absolutely broken the law with several issues and I want to know which one you would like to address first:

1. Sexual Harassment
2. Violation of privacy regarding your academic records
3. Violation of privacy concerning your health

I gained some comfort in learning my suspicions were correct. Although I really didn't know much about all of this, I did know how Jackson's actions and comments made me feel. I knew I was "low man on the totem pole" in the chain of command, but I knew the way I was being treated was inappropriate and wrong. I was allowing him to take my power and strength from me, and I had to make him stop!

I clearly stated my desire: "I am not here to take legal action towards the university, I just want this man to leave me alone and stop harassing me. I just want to do my job and be allowed to continue taking classes during the day. I also want to stop being made to feel guilty about having had cancer, and just for the record, it did not slow me down. I want to be valued as an employee, and continue my education.

My job benefits not only affect me, but my entire family. I was overcome with emotion and began to weep. All I could say in that moment was, "I just can't take the disrespect and I know when he reads my email about my talking to Walter, there will be horrible repercussions towards my actions to make him stop."

Stephanie specifically instructed me on how to respond if Jackson continued the verbal abuse. The information I received from her coincided with my instincts, as she coached me on how to handle his future outburst and demands. This was a source of strength for me, and I was somewhat surprised that a university employee was being an advocate for me. I suspect that many HR Managers would have towed the company line.

I learned so much from her that day, but the most important knowledge I gained was that I was not the crazy one. Jackson's behavior was out of line and now I had confirmation. Stephanie advised me to do my job and call her immediately upon another confrontation, and that she would take the necessary steps to diffuse the situation.

Returning to my desk, I was concerned I would be asked about where I had been so immediately I dove into my daily responsibilities.

I was interrupted with what I now refer to as a "life changing" phone call. As I picked up the receiver I was taken surprised by Jackson's voice on the other end calling from another state. In a casual introduction he light-heartedly asked me, "What's happening?" I was caught off guard by the timing of his call having just confided in Stephanie about Jackson's behavior. Was I just being suspicious and paranoid, or did he actually have knowledge of my HR visit? Did someone tip him off to my meeting?

I updated him on the progress of my daily work and he immediately steered the conversation towards the upcoming academic meeting. He confirmed the logistical details of the meeting along with confirming those who would be attending.

Just as Stephanie from HR had coached me, I slowly recited the phrases she had offered while concentrating on the appropriate wording, and politely decline his attendance at the meeting. I calmly stated my reason for him not to be present, as I thanked him for his effort and assured him that I would give him a specific summary of my academic plan. He boldly interrupted me, and I could feel the heat rising within my body due to the stress. He went into a complete rage, telling me he was not going to be cut out of this f*****g deal and it was because of him that I had this academic appointment. I didn't ask for assistance with this matter and frankly I considered it an intrusion in my personal life. Jackson continued his rage by taking the Lord's name in vain multiple times along with additional profanity. I asked him to stop using the inappropriate language. I calmly but confidently said, "Stop talking to me like that, and please stop disrespecting me. You will not disrespect me like that!"

I verbally recited to him what Stephanie advised me to say. I firmly proclaimed, "I am not comfortable with you seeing my academic records and it makes me uncomfortable for you to be at this meeting. I invited my current advisor Caroline Wilson to be present, and the three of us (including Mark Hamilton) will discuss my degree plan." He angrily replied, "I am going to this meeting!" Jackson's voice was at a high pitch and I could feel his anger burning through the phone line.

At this point my defense mechanisms had kicked in and I abandoned the calm, tactful script Stephanie had given me. I boldly responded,

"No, you are not attending this meeting. I have spoken to HR and it is my decision. I do not want you there."

All of a sudden Jackson stopped the conversation. It was as if a light flashed before his eyes as he gathered his thoughts. I could tell he was regaining control of his thoughts and temper. Perhaps my "meeting with HR" comment sunk in. The abuse came to a sudden halt.

I redirected the conversation to the day's activities in the office and told him we would discuss this further when he returned to town. I hung up the phone I dialed HR and informed Stephanie Brown of the specific details of our conversation. She applauded me for taking a stand. "It is time to shut him down," she said. It was at that moment I realized the magnitude of this situation and the type of man I was dealing with. As I stretched my "shaking" body, I was rushed by several concerned colleagues who had overheard the conversation. I had not realized the volume of my voice and the drama the conversation was attracting to others. Nevertheless, it was to my advantage to have witnesses to this very troubling situation.

The following day, I sent Jackson confirmation of the upcoming academic meeting with the individuals of whom would be present:

From: Woodson, Nancy
Sent: Thursday, June 22, 2006
To: Hyde, Jackson
Subject: Friday

Jackson,
I received your message and I have the meeting down at 10:30 in his office. I have asked my advisor to join the meeting and I am hoping the three of us (Mark, Nancy and Caroline) can develop a strategy. I will keep you posted.
Thanks,
Nancy Woodson
Donor Club

The meeting was extremely helpful towards my academic course and Mark proved to be a valuable resource and allied in the future.

Leake Family 1984 (My Rehearsal Dinner)
Front Row – Steve (deceased), Dad, Mother, Pat & Tim
Back Row – Kristen, Terry (deceased), Nancy, Susanne & Cindy

Woodson Family 2006
Seated - Sam, Lawrence, Bailey, Carrie, Jo Ann (deceased) & Pat
Standing – Nancy, Jay, Doug, Patrick & Olivia
… Not Pictured – Chad and Ben

Lawrence's 1st Day of Boarding School
August 2008

Nancy, Jay, Bailey
Doug and Lawrence

Cancer Free Party – 2006

Jay's Senior Year with Grandparents

Bailey, Lawrence and Jay – 2009

Bailey's Graduation Party with Lawrence and Cary

Doug and Nancy

Lawrence and Chief

CHAPTER 13
This is Not Good

A NAGGING TWINGE OF NAUSEA WAS beginning to increase in my stomach, and I developed an intense, sharp pain in my upper abdomen. After months of pain control with inconsistent results my doctor determined my gallbladder should be removed. The procedure itself did not concern me, but I was insecure about being judged by others because many fellow employees were aware of my previous health related absences. I knew my "sick time" and "vacation time" were mine to take, but I wanted to check with HR regarding my legal rights on providing specific information to my employer.

(sic)
From: Woodson, Nancy
Sent: Thursday, September 21, 2006
To: Brown, Stephanie
Subject: FW: Doctor's Appointment/Other

Stephanie,
Once again....how much health information am I obligated to give Jackson regarding my doctor appointment? I have already turned in my sick hours for this visit on the 26th and I thought informing him I would be gone was the "thing" to do. Thoughts?
Nancy

Stephanie confirmed my thinking with this specific information:

(sic)
From: Brown, Stephanie
Sent: Thu 9/21/2006
Subject: RE: Doctor's Appointment/Other

You are not obligated/required to divulge any personal/health information to your manager.

I anticipated my private information was my business and not disclosing my personal information was protected by the law, but wanted to make sure. It was my fourth surgery in fourteen months, and I was hoping it would be the last. Time was flying by with family, work, and school. The Thanksgiving holiday weekend was coming to a close and I was gearing up for the month-long Christmas celebration. As I prepared my mind to organize my "to do" list, I could feel myself entering the "It's Business" mode.

Balancing my school work with business was often a challenge, but with careful planning and calculations, I had my schedule down to every hour of each day. Everything was seemingly moving according to plan when the unexpected entered my world again.

It was a Thursday, December 9th and our work staff was preparing for another seated luncheon. Forty-five minutes before the paid guests were to arrive we were anxiously waiting for the maintenance crew to arrive to the room and set up the tables and chairs. The administrative assistant frantically made three calls to Jackson and each time he assured her that he would be arriving soon to assist. With only twenty minutes left before the event was to start she decided our staff, of four women must set up the room for the expected crowd. Three older men, who worked in the building kindly, offered their assistance to quickly transform the room. We all worked fast pulling the tables and chairs for 250 people out of the storage closest and arranged them in banquet style.

Being somewhat of a weakling I cautiously started lifting and moving while decreasing the weight limit with each trip. I confessed to one of the men that I had to be the weakest person in the room. We both laughed and made light of the situation as perspiration poured from our foreheads. Even though it wasn't our responsibility to set up the room we worked frantically to get this done and save a lot of embarrassment.

The room took on a miraculous change in appearance. I was convinced that I had fulfilled my workout requirement for the day and maybe for the week! The room was ready to go only a few minutes prior to the start time as Jackson arrived.

The luncheon was a success. Within a few hours, I experienced a nagging ache in my right arm. Not paying much attention to the discomfort, the pain grew with intensity during the following week. I made a comment in passing to one my colleagues about the pain but wasn't really thinking much of it.

The following weekend included multiple parties to start the holiday season. I decided to take a short nap on a Saturday afternoon, so I would be well rested for the evening. When I woke up, the strangest thing occurred... I had lost mobility and feeling in my 3rd, 4th and 5th fingers of my right hand. This was puzzling but I really wasn't too concerned. I figured I had slept on it wrong, and it would take a few minutes for the circulation to return. As the afternoon wore on the mobility did not return and I started to worry somewhat. As I got dressed for the evening I found it impossible to apply my makeup. Opting for a more natural look, Doug and I left for the party. I placed a shawl over my shoulders and placed my right hand underneath it as a new disguise. As the evening progressed, I anxiously waited for the feeling to return, but no improvement.

We attended a sit down dinner and my right handedness made this a bit challenging. The paralysis in my right hand proved to be difficult. I tried my best not to drop my fork while balancing my wrap. Too often we take things for granted and do not realize how important something is until it is lost.

The night came to an end and I was exhausted from trying to keep my strange secret. I could not share yet another health issue with anyone and for sure could not talk about it. What would I say? I took a nap and woke up with a parallelized hand. It sounded like a movie on the Lifetime channel.

The next morning as soon as I awoke up, I immediately checked for the return of motion only to be terribly disappointed. The motion had not restored itself and, in fact, I felt like it had worsened. I remember a strong feeling of disbelief that this was happening and I felt like something was really wrong. My first thought was I maybe having a stroke. I calmly entered my "It's Business" mode by executing the day's plan in my head.

It was 7:45 on a Sunday morning and my house was still asleep. I wasn't sure what to do, so I decided to drive myself to the emergency room. I was reluctant to enter another hospital door, but I knew it would be irresponsible if it was something and I didn't address it.

I threw on my sweats and grabbed a few items to pass the time during the big wait. I thought it best not to wake the sleeping husband, but soon changed my mind thinking he probably should know my where-abouts. I really did not want to burden him again with the hospital scene. Doug had spent enough time in the hard chairs staring at the stark floors and enduring the indescribable stagnant.

I quietly whispered that I was heading out the door to the emergency room, just to make sure I was not having a stroke. As his eye opened he calmly asked if I wanted him to go. It was kind of him to offer, but I told him I would rather be by myself. I really did not want to go either, but I had a feeling tugging on me that something was wrong.

As I entered the ER in my daughter's pink, sweat suit with coffee in hand I casually approached the reception window: "I am not sure if I really should be here, but I have lost movement in three of my fingers and I want to make sure I am not having a stroke." The nurse immediately rushed me in from behind the counter. After taking all my vital signs she ushered me into a 3x5 area with a sliding curtain.

I was pleasantly surprised that I was moving in the system so quickly only to be sadly disappointed hours later. One by one I was approached by multiple, personnel asked to tell my story and asked the same questions. After several hours, my I-pod shuffle had run out of juice and I had already memorized the articles in my magazine because I had read them so many times.

I felt as if the small room surrounded by the curtain was closing in on me and the stinch of the vomit from the adjacent area completely nauseated me. I was cursing my sinus doctor for renewing my sense of smell. I overheard many conversations and multiple voices focusing on their problems. I listened to their aches and ailments and was reminded that my problems were small. I was grateful for my life and this hospital trip served as a reminder to how blessed I was. My outlook immediately changed when I overheard a man on the phone. He was speaking of his pending absence from work in the days ahead because he wanted to attend his daughter's rape trial. My jaw dropped in disbelief as I heard the conversation. I was ready to get the hell out of that hospital so I quickly jumped up, dressed myself and pulled back the curtain to force the issue of my release. A male nurse entered my area. As I placed my jacket over my shoulders I began to cry. "I have been here, for over seven hours and I've been left alone for over three; I have to get out of here," I told the RN. He calmly encouraged me to settle down and within minutes the x-ray machine arrived to conduct the final necessary tests. The cause of my finger paralysis was unclear. The doctor suggested that I be admitted to the hospital for additional tests. By this time I had been in the ER for over eight hours combined with having missed a mother/daughter tea. I finally negotiated my release on the condition that I would call the recommended neurologist and make an appointment the following day. As I left the hospital in my germy pink suit, all I could dream of was taking a shower and being able to move and use my right fingers again.

The next morning, I called the doctor's office and they informed me of an appointment which I had already missed. I jumped into the car and headed straight to her office. She was a lovely lady, but she was stumped as to the reason for my injury as well. She ordered additional tests, but the radiologist's office was unable to accommodate further testing until the end of the week. The doctor placed me on steroids hoping to reduce any swelling. I was feeling the stress of missing work, but I did communicate updates as they became available. The problem was I rarely had anything notable to report, except that I was injured, not sure how, not sure why and what was Hurt, only that I had lost motion in three fingers. I returned to work the following day and basically kept my right arm in my lap. I typed with my left hand button by button, hunting and pecking.

The results from the MRI offered little explanation for the immobility and loss of sensation. With classes starting in just four weeks I felt an urgency to be proactive regarding a diagnosis. I called several friends and asked for assistance in getting an appointment with a hand surgeon gave me a name and number and fortunately there was a cancellation the following day and the doctor graciously agreed to see me.

Doug accompanied me on my first visit. He was concerned about my state of mind… or perhaps my lack thereof. The steroids were a contributing factor to my crying attacks and the reality of my paralysis was starting to wear thin on my emotions. I was tired and just wanted to return to the simple pleasures of life such as opening a door, putting on lipstick or writing my name.

The doctor entered the room and made his diagnosis. He believed it was the result of an injury and was certain the motion would return within six weeks. I was surprised and devastated. I tearfully informed him I didn't have six weeks as class was starting in less than three. I tried to explain my strong female intuition. I continued by telling him that I thought I would need surgery to repair the injury. Doug sat in silence shaking his head, but not in disbelief. Once again he found himself in that familiar place… should he support the medical expert or the crazy wife? It was a toss-up, but we both decided to support the medical expert. The doctor told me he wanted to see me the following week to track my progress and assured me he was confident in his diagnosis. He ordered additional testing with a nerve doctor to pinpoint the specific damaged area.

Christmas was fast approaching and lucky for me I had completed my shopping a few days before at the beginning of the month. My sister Terry had offered to make my Christmas dinner for our family and meticulously planned out the entire menu. I invited her family to join the Woodson celebration, but she declined. Terry was increasingly making excuses for not leaving her house and had embarrassed about her weight gain.

Doug called a family meeting with Bailey, Jay and Lawrence and asked for family cooperation with the holiday chores and entertaining. My dining room had been set for weeks for Christmas Day as part of my holiday decorations, but warming up the dinner and executing the meal required some work. Bailey confidently took on the role of top chef with an apron on her waist and a drill sergeant's control of the kitchen.

I continued to orchestrate the details by offering multiple "suggestions" for the busy holiday. The big meal was scheduled for 12:00. My in-laws arrived promptly at 11:30 am. In spite of the demanding Christmas Day with our family was wonderful. The meal was delicious and the time spent together was precious. I was so proud of Doug, and my children for handling the Christmas details, that I was unable to physically accomplish.

The following week I returned to the hand surgeon's office. The doctor entered the room and kindly asked about my progress. I carefully pointed to the additional numbness in two previously unaffected fingers and an additional loss of motion. He exited the room to call the nerve doctor as he asked for the specific location of the damaged nerve. The nerve test revealed trauma in the right forearm and the damaged nerve was interrupting the nerve connectors to my fingers. The doctor confidently looked at me and said, "You were right, we need to operate." I pointed out that it would be best to do this right away. "If you are going to operate, it would be for insurance deductable reasons. In addition, my class schedule starts back up in three weeks."

The doctor amazingly consented to my request. He instructed me to meet him at the surgery center the following morning. "We are taking care of this tomorrow," he said, "I will see you at 7:30." For the first time I was excited about a surgery. My female intuition told me it needed to be done, the clock was ticking, and I needed to get on with my recovery, my work and my new semester courses.

I called Doug from the office to inform him of the surgery. He was surprised by the doctor's change in treatment, but was encouraged by his optimistic attitude.

We arrived at the hospital very early in the morning for another pre-operative process. The IV stick was not successful until the third attempt, and I vividly remember looking into Doug's eyes during the last stick. He could tell what I was thinking, "I am so done with this whole surgery thing." With five surgeries in less than two years, I had earned that right. And besides, not one of those surgeries was of a cosmetic nature!

It was hard being home for the three weeks that followed the surgery. I followed HR procedures with all correspondence and reminded myself daily of the words from Stephanie Brown, "You are not required to divulge any health information." Even so, I felt it was important to communicate my progress. I stopped by the HR office one day with paper work from my doctor and Stephanie told me I would not be allowed to come back until the stitches were removed on January 11th. I know she was allowing me emotional and physical time to heal as I would have forced myself to go back to work. I was relieved when I left her office, because I was given a license to rest.

The truth is: I was dreaded to go back to work under Jackson. I was tired of living the charade of the "happy employee." Jackson's inappropriate language and demands killed my motivation. I was too old to lift tables and too tired to attend 60 events. The extra expectations combined with going to class and taking care of a family was just too much. My home life and my work life was starting to feel unbalance, as I was completely feeling defeated. I was tired of feeling guilty for having a family and trying to earn my degree. The balancing act had come to an end in my mind and I saw my paralyzed hand as a sign to make some major changes for my emotional and physical sanity. I knew something would need to change and change fast. I felt as if I was losing my confidence at work, not because of my efforts, but by the way I was treated. My patience became short with my children, and twice I escaped to my closet for peace and solitude during the holiday probably due to the office stress that I brought home with me.

CHAPTER 14
The Truth Will Set You Free

MY HOLIDAY RECUPERATION TIME ALLOWED me the opportunity to reflect on the dysfunctional work environment I found myself in. I knew something had to change and that I must be the one to request that change. One night it suddenly struck me the time had come to ask for a job transfer. The stress of working under Jackson had compromised my confidence and damaged my spirit and possibly was having an adverse impact on my health. I had four surgeries while working under his supervision and his attitude and actions were counterproductive. Shameful language, disrespectful emails and unreasonable demands had become a pattern of behavior that I could no longer tolerate. I decided to send an email to Eugene Dunkas, the Vice Chancellor, to request an immediate transfer. I knew I was not going through the proper chain of command, but I wanted this situation remedied promptly. I had followed procedures in the recent months, requesting assistance to deal with the disrespectful behavior, but the process had not produced any positive change. I wanted out and I was ready to say it out loud. I did not tell Doug, or anyone else, that I was setting the wheels in motion. This was my decision, and I did not want to be influenced by alternative opinions. There were risks associated with my request, but in my mind staying in an abusive work environment was far more detrimental so I sent an email:

To: Dunkas, Eugene
From: Woodson, Nancy
Date: January 3, 2007
Subject: Woodson

Eugene,
I need to meet with you asap off campus....we have much to discuss - long overdue.

As I touched the send button I had initiated a process that could have catastrophic consequences. The medical benefits were of great value to our family and my existing condition would make it difficult to obtain insurance. In addition to the tuition benefit risking the loss of tuition benefits for my children and me. I had invested countless hours of hard work and spent time away from my family and friends, but I decided I must stand up for my dignity and self respect. This was most important to me and for the example I was setting for my children. My family participated in many of the discussions regarding Jackson's behavior. A valuable lesson was being learned by all of us; never tolerate anyone speaking to you in a disrespectful way. I knew deep inside my heart that I had to stand up for myself because no one else was going to do it for me.

Eugene responded to my email a few days later and inquired about the nature of the meeting I had requested. I assumed he was questioning my agenda and I suspect he wondered if it was related to my arm injury that occurred on campus. I did not offer any information so as not to upstage our meeting and immediately received confirmation on a time and location for the meeting. I felt confident with my course of action. I practiced my words over and over in my head, never once doubting my decision to ask for a transfer. I chose not to speak to anyone about the meeting or the upcoming conversation. I was probably being overly cautious because over the past fourteen months my husband, family and friends had told me to let everything roll off my shoulders and just do my job. Time and time again, I was reminded of the benefits of my job, but I had decided that this environment had become toxic and was adversely affecting my mental and physical health. I truly believe if I had been a single mother with three children I would never had never taken a stand. I would have continued doing my job despite the situation and not revealed this mistreatment to my colleagues. I had a husband who could provide for me if my job was lost and that gave me courage to do what I knew was right. Part of my motivation in telling my story is to empower those who feel that they cannot right a wrong for fear of reprisal.

I did have an undercover support group on campus consisting of my two academic advisors and Stephanie Brown from Human Resources. I kept a notebook full emails, memos and notes from day one not knowing how beneficial it would become. I was ready to move forward; I had had enough. My plan was to take the high road by diplomatically revealing Jackson's inappropriate conduct and suggesting that a transfer was the best course of action.

As I entered Eugene's office it was bothersome that I couldn't gracefully remove my coat due to the multiple strings that supported my paralyzed fingers....way too much effort. In a strictly professional manner, Eugene asked me the nature of the meeting. I calmly requested to be relocated from my current position to another department on campus. Without offering any details of the work environment, I stated: "This position has not been a good fit for me, and I think I can do more for the university if I am doing what I was hired to do." With a blank and confused look on his face he calmly inquired about the real reason for my meeting request. He asked me if something had happened in the work environment. Being very guarded and selective with my words, I calmly stated that something had happened, but I was not here to speak of the incidents. I was here to offer a solution and reiterate my commitment to my work. I was not interested in office politics, I just wanted to do my job to do it well and go home to my family each day. My positive statements took him by surprise because he knew something was wrong. He didn't know what it was so he kept the conversation brief. He asked my permission to speak with Jackson about my request and I hesitantly agreed. I closed the meeting by stating I was not there to speak of the details of the situation, but I had enough. While clinching my coat while trying to adjust my fallen coat over the custom made apparatus, I tried not to lose eye contact while guarding my injured arm. I was confident in my request and reminded myself not to over stay my welcome. I immediately went back to my office and jumped back into my one-arm work routine. I felt as if I were leading a double life with my office team because I was trying to escape from the group. No one knew about my request and my hope was to quietly transfer to another position. This was the path of least resistance; at the time I was convinced of that, but boy was I wrong. Little did I know the reaction and retaliation my request would bring.

Another annual performance review was approaching and not thinking much of it, I casually entered the meeting totally unprepared for what ensued. Jackson had his assistant present which was unconventional but I didn't mind. The final step in this yearly process was for me to sign the written evaluation the supervisor typically completed within a few days of our meeting.

The next day, Jackson hurriedly came into my office and handed me the written report. He asked me to sign the evaluation and return it to his assistant within the hour. I thanked him and he headed out the door on a Friday afternoon.

As I read the evaluation, my mouth dropped and I could feel the temperature rising in my body. The paper became heavier with the turning of each page. I read the words in disbelief. Nothing contained in the pages remotely resembled anything we had discussed in our meeting the day before. Not only did he criticize the quality of my work, he attacked me personally. Neither his opinions nor his analysis were accurate. It was as if he was describing someone else. Every employee on our team was required to keep meticulous records of each meeting and the outcome. My reports were complete and my results were strong. His production was recorded monthly like the rest of us, it revealed little activity and miniscule giving results. All I could figure was someone must be protecting him, as he was not being held to the same standard as the rest of us.

I walked into the assistant's office and burst into tears. I was overwhelmed with emotional exhaustion as I couldn't believe how all my hard work was being discredited, by an inexperienced supervisor. I gathered my thoughts and shared with her his abusive and demanding conduct over the last fourteen months. She shared with me a similar situation she experienced with an older alumni, where a university supporter called her a bitch during an emotional outburst. She encouraged me not to accept his poor evaluation, but to go back and document my performance. I thanked her and decided to proceed in the manner she suggested.

I returned to my office to phone a colleague in the research department to request my production records from the last twelve months. It was a Friday afternoon approaching five o'clock, and she offered to stay late to retrieve the necessary information. She could sense the anxiety in my voice and asked me what the problem was. I simply told her I had to defend my production and she offered her assistance.

The wheels were turning over the weekend as I prepared a three-page rebuttal to my 12-month review. My report contained detailed documentation in support of my strong production from the previous year.

By the following Monday morning, I was ready to present my case. I had prepared two copies, one for Jackson and one for his assistant. The assistant complimented me on my efforts and encouraged me to request a meeting for the three of us.

I approached his office Jackson was sitting in the chair across from his desk because as an IT person was working on his computer. I was a little thrown off by his physical location in the room typically because he is seated behind his desk. I handed him the folder with the following report and cheerfully said "good morning."

I am requesting an opportunity to discuss my review to what I consider to be an inaccurate evaluation. As I reached out to hand him my folder, he defiantly declined to accept the paperwork and told me to take it out of his office. I reiterated that he might want to review the material for our upcoming meeting, so we could discuss my rebuttal in detail. He looked at me with a deep stare as if he was looking right through me and told me he knew what was in the folder and he was not interested in it at all. Needless to say, that was not the response I expected. Stunned, I insisted he view the information for our upcoming meeting that I hoped to have and he abruptly told me to leave his office. I wasn't really sure how to respond, so I just turned and walked away.

January 29, 2007

Mr. Jackson Hyde
666 Disappointing Street
Somewhere, Texas 00000

Dear Mr. Hyde,

Thank you for the time you allowed out of your day last Thursday, January 25th for my annual review. I appreciate the detailed discussion I had with you and your assistant regarding the last twelve months of my job performance, and hearing your future vision for my position as a Campus Officer.

After my review of your written report on my overall performance, I am requesting that you consider re-evaluating my performance with a revised copy. It is my opinion that your assessment does not accurately grade my overall performance...

I have also enclosed an itemized list of all client entries from the last twelve months for you to view as daily and monthly entries. I have been very diligent in my work with our organization and have been very proud of what I have brought to the organization.

Thank you for your consideration.

Sincerely,
Nancy Woodson
Cc: Assistant

I went straight to his assistant's office. "What did you tell him?" I breathlessly asked her. She responded, "Nothing." She told me she had not spoken to him since Friday afternoon. She immediately offered to speak with him to evaluate the situation.

I returned to my office feeling somewhat panicked. Within minutes, she came around the corner and requested a time for an afternoon meeting. I was experiencing a small panic attack, but was confident in my professional ability to handle this situation.

The meeting was scheduled for two o'clock, which made for a long couple of hours. As I entered Jackson's office once again, he and the department assistant were present. I sat in the chair across from his desk. The mood was dark inside but the sun was paring through the window. I pulled the folder from my lap and as I was lifting it towards the desktop, Jackson abruptly started the meeting with a rhetorical question.

"Guess where I was on Friday afternoon? Well, I will tell you where I was" he replied. "I was up the hill for my review and for twenty minutes we talked about how Nancy Woodson has been up the hill telling the head guy that she is not happy in this position and she wants out. So my whole review was talking about you and by the way - how dare you go behind my back, but most of all how dare you go behind Walter's back, our superior. He is the one that hired you. This is not how we do things at this university and if you were not happy with your work conditions, then you should have come to me."

I looked at him right in the eyes and firmly stated, "I did come to you and I asked you to respect me and our team by changing your vulgar language and your constant harassment regarding my class schedule and my physical health. After you used the word 'dick' four times in our staff meeting and used the 'f' word both verbally and in documentation and continued taking the Lord's name in vain, I finally decided our team needed help in dealing with your constant mood swings. It was only after those occasions that I decided to go to HR. When you prevented me from taking classes during the day by telling me it was your call, not mine (or anyone else's) including my previous employer, then yes, I went to Walter and asked for his assistance. "But the most degrading thing you continued to do is make me feel guilty for having cancer. In the first two months you were here, you brought up my disease in my review and told me cancer had slowed me down… and by the way, it didn't." I was shaking but the words continued to flow from my mouth and I firmly stated, "you probably don't even know you have broken the law in several areas?"

- Asking an employee for her personal health information
- Demanding my academic information

- Sexual harassment with vulgar language, both verbally and electronically

"When I never received any kind of response from your superior for help with you, I then contacted HR for assistance and documented all your disrespectful actions toward me and our team. Finally, after being injured and recovering from surgery over the 2007 Christmas holiday, I decided this position was not a good fit for me and I approached the Vice Chancellor with a request for a job transfer. I went to him to defend my production and work ethic. I did not go to him to address your harassment. You even had the nerve to put your abuse in an email."

Jackson quickly denied ever writing any derogatory words and sending me any kind of electronic message. I continued to stare directly into his eyes as I said, "The soft copy is saved on my blackberry and the hard copy is home in my underwear drawer. If you would like, I would be happy to get it for you so we can refresh your memory." His demeanor changed instantly and he took on a "deer in the head lights" look as he reiterated his denial in writing such a message. I confidently offered to show him the "saved" message, but he declined. I had a strong sense that alcohol played a role in his writing and sending the vile message as the content was angry and full of misspelled words:

From: Hyde, Jackson
Sent: Tue 6/20/2006
To: Woodson, Nancy

(sic)
I want to know what the hell is going on with you and if there is something going on with you health I want to hear from you and not from others in thisv office.
I made this appt. And I will be going and will not be cut out damn it. F- bomb!
I have spoke to hour everyday and checked on the regulations.... response...so you will know I have spoken to HR too!
I am the Director ... and I will will tell you how you will spending time during my schedule. It is my call and it is up to me if you sill take classes during the day.

I was shocked at what I had just said. I couldn't believe that I had so bravely and rifled off confidently such a strong defense. I was amazed at the inner strength that came out of no where allowing me to stand face to face with my abuser while having little fear and no regret. I had so much at stake by taking such a stand, but I knew that if I did not defend my self-respect, and integrity was much more important than my job and its benefits.

While raising his voice Jackson said, "I told you I was sorry." I strongly replied, "No, you didn't." He instantly snapped, "Yes, I did!" I reiterated, "No, you did not apologize and that is what this is all about." He stopped and lowered his voice and said, "Then let me say I apologize." I calmly stated: "I accept your apology - thank you." I don't believe his words were heartfelt, but I was grateful for the apology because it diffused the stressful situation.

The mood of the conversation suddenly changed as my superior took control of the dialogue. "Fine, you want out....you will be out. I will be in charge of your job relocation on campus, along with Christopher Rhodes and Walter Phillips." The two colleagues to whom he referred were both of our superiors. In the chain of command, both Jackson and I reported to them. "The four of us will sit down and discuss your options and what is available on campus." His tone and attitude took on a kinder nature and the meeting ended in a professional manner. I asked him if we were okay and he responded "yes." Concluding the conversation and exiting his office was quite a relief. I bought in to his lie, totally unsuspecting of the retaliation that he had in stored for me.

CHAPTER 15

Extremes are Dangerous

THE DAYS IN THE OFFICE continued at a rapid pace and the previous office drama was not discussed between the team. The wheels of my transition were in motion but at a snail's pace. Jackson and I put up a good front before the other staff members, but I knew everyone could feel the tension.

The annual "Signing Day" event was approaching announcing the newly signed football players for the upcoming fall season. As the Donor Club prepared for the reception at a local country club the office was in full planning mode preparing to host the sold-out event. I found myself feeling self-conscious and uneasy in such a disrespectful environment. I felt somewhat paranoid wondering if others had knowledge or were whispering about the ongoing dispute.

Standing alone most of the evening I was approached by the university's Marketing Director, Michael Simms. Mike approached me and engaged me in a casual conversation. Out of the blue, he curiously asked me why I had a chip on my shoulder with my boss, Jackson Hyde. Surprised by his comment, I confidently replied, "I don't have a chip on my shoulder, but I do have a problem with his disrespect." I was standing before this man in fear and desperately wanted him to know the truth about what I had experienced. However, I made a conscious decision not to speak of the conflict. I was secretly shaking inside as his words confirmed my suspicions of the internal gossip. I knew the "boys club" existed but I also knew in my heart my stand was the right thing to do, even if few people knew the truth. I constantly had to remind myself that the truth will someday set me free.

As I casually moved to another location in the crowded room, I remember leaning against an indoor pillar for support. This event seemed to be never ending when suddenly I was approached by the president of the volunteer organization. He surprisingly shared with me his knowledge of Jackson's abusive behavior and language and said he was in disbelief of his conduct. He kindly told me I had done a good job in my current position and encouraged me to "cheer up and smile."

Cheer up and smile? Please. Being cheerful in my situation was unconscionable and a smile at this moment in my life was about the last thing I was able to do. My suspicions of being a "marked" employee had been validated but limiting my chatter to others would be beneficial to my future.

After the President's comment, I realized I must have looked uncomfortable in my surroundings but I was grateful that a few people secretly supported my stand. Deep down I wanted to immediately leave the event, knowing my time was limited with this organization. I felt like a fraud pretending to be part of the team. The whole thing just disgusted me. Laws had been broken, but being able to prove the abuse would require patience and time on my part. I continued to play the part of the devoted employee because I had an agenda for my family. I had to stay focused on the end goal; be removed from the hostile work environment, do my job and do it well.

I compared myself to my daughter Bailey's running of the hurdles in a middle school track meet years ago. Each wooden hurdle represented the many life challenges ahead.

With every step, I was gaining confidence and strength. I could feel the increasing momentum with each obstacle as my heart pounded with the increasing momentum. I was starting to feel my personal rhythm connect with the timing of my footsteps between each wooden stand. My race was maximizing to full speed and I knew in my heart I was doing the right thing - standing up to this man and his abusive behavior. I knew I had to defend my right for my education and if that meant losing my job and the chance for my degree, then I was prepared for the consequences of my actions. I found it personally fascinating that I never once regretted my strides with this institution. With each day I felt empowered by my renewed strength. I knew God had His hand in this situation because I intuitively felt the correct course of action. I knew "time" would be on my side and I needed to stay focused on the goal.....or the finish line of the race.

Every morning I coached myself to walk into my office with a positive attitude. It was a struggle to be mentally and physically efficient with the fear of having to speak with Jackson. Just seeing his face and having to pretend nothing was wrong made me feel terribly uncomfortable.

Stephanie was continuing to update me with information as it became available. However; the days turned into weeks and conversations were less frequent. The Vice Chancellor's busy schedule prevented him from focusing on my relocation. Stephanie checked on me sporadically and I assured her I was able to continue my duties. One day I received an unexpected request from Jackson:

From: Hyde, Jackson
Sent: Tue 2/20/2007
To: Woodson, Nancy
RE: Organizational Card

The Card should have at least 100 companies on board by the end of the fiscal year – those are the kinds of goals we should have for it.
See me with any questions
Thanks

Jackson's goal for me to obtain a total of 100 sponsor members was an unreasonable expectation. It had taken twelve months to commit 42 businesses and now in three months he was asking me to add another fifty-eight? Clearly he was trying to set me up for failure by giving me an unrealistic goal, so I responded with this reasonable request:

From: Woodson, Nancy
Sent: Tue 2/20/2007
To: Hyde, Jackson
RE: Donor Card

"The Card should have at least 100 companies on board by the end

of the fiscal year – those are the kinds of goals we should have for it"... That would be great but I think very unrealistic by myself. I have approached almost 100 merchants and have 42 signed up. Maybe we should divide your goals of the additional 60 new merchants by the three of us... each of us needs to sign up 20 new merchants by June 1st. Working together the Donor Club would accomplish an additional 60 participants. That is really the only way to achieve those kinds of numbers. ..
Thanks!
N

He had no interest in working together to complete this unrealistic goal.

From: Hyde, Jackson
Sent: Tue 2/21/2007
To: Woodson, Nancy
RE: Organizational Card

We can visit on it later today.
I also update you efforts that are ongoing regarding your request to Eugene and I for a move to another department. There are some things that will require your efforts.
JH

I was anxious to hear the new developments from Jackson so I immediately knocked on his office door and requested an update regarding my job transition. Over the past weeks we had few conversations, but the ones we had were professional and courteous. Jackson was speaking on the phone, but he motioned me with a wave in the air to enter his office. I entered his office and shut the door quietly as he was finishing his conversation. I sat across from his desk in the same chair from the previous conflict. I listened as he gallantly stated the update.

"As of now, there is not a position available in our department," Jackson said and "your job will be terminated as of May 31st." Jackson handed me a typed memo from the Associate Vice Chancellor, Christopher Rhodes, on university stationery, stating my termination from the Donor Club on May 31, 2007.

MEMORANDUM

TO: Jackson Hyde
CC: Nancy Woodson
FROM: Christopher Rhodes
DATE: February 21, 2007
RE: Transition Plan for Nancy Woodson

It has come to my attention through discussion with Walter that Nancy Woodson would like to transition out of her position on the Donor Club staff. I understand you and she have discussed this thoroughly and have agreed on a transition plan. The plan as I understand it is for Nancy to secure another position by the end of the fiscal year, May 31, 2007.

This memo is to let you know that I am aware of this situation and I support the timeline on which you and Nancy have agreed. In addition, I support our working with Nancy to explore other options on campus in hopes that another position at the University might be more suitable for her.

Please let me know if there is anything else I can do to assist in the process.

Within seconds panic spread through my body. I explained to Jackson that I was not aware of this agreement, and he assured me it was a mutual decision between Christopher and the HR department. He informed me Eugene had turned this transition over to Christopher and now he (Jackson) was heading my reassignment. "No one else is spending time with your job relocation; in fact, I am the one handling it. I am in charge of your repositioning and I am telling you again there is nothing for you in this department," he said. I politely asked if I could meet with Christopher to discuss my options. He firmly said, "No."

It is almost March," Jackson added, "I suggest you look at the HR website to see what is available. You have two kids needing that tuition benefit isn't that correct?" "Yes," I replied. He looked at me and snidely said "You better get busy!" All of a sudden, with a condescendingly evil stare he pulled out an internal community newsletter, slapped it down on the desk and said, "Oh look, there is a job for a painter or a landscaper; maybe you could become a painter or work in the physical plant. Here is a newsletter with the job postings on campus; maybe this will give you some ideas."

I asked Jackson if I could have a copy of the memo and newsletter. He told me it was mine to take. At that moment I knew the time had come to protect myself and my family. My theories were confirmed at that moment of his bullying episodes and unethical behavior.

> *I was starting to feel an unbalance in my step. The rhythm from my legs to my brain was starting to disconnect. My shoestring became my enemy and I could feel my legs starting to crumble in slow motion. I knew I was falling, I could feel the heat from the ground coming closer to my face. Suddenly, I threw my hands to catch my disoriented body. I found myself powerless to break my fall. I had to just let my body crash. I heard the crack of the broken bone in my right arm, as I knew I had to hit bottom before rising to the top.*

My options with this man were exhausted and the best thing for me to do was to thank him for his time and exit his office. I was very concerned about what all this meant. Was the system protecting me or failing me? What just happened and how did it happen? Did I just lose my job because I stood up to my abuser and to the system?

Jackson Hyde resembled the infamous Jekyll & Hyde character. Jackson and J&H have similar characteristics, as their personal attacks are vicious and vindictive in private, but innocent and charming in front of witnesses. People who knew him find it difficult to believe he was capable of such disrespectful and aggressive behavior. The people abused by him have seen the real Jackson, of the J&H fame.

Jackson concluded the meeting by abruptly stating, "That's all." I thanked him for the update and left his office. I walked into my office, picked up my belongings and left the building. As I walked to the car, I called and left a voicemail message for Stephanie Brown in HR requesting an immediate meeting. I walked into Stephanie's office and immediately broke down. I showed her the memo from Christopher Rhodes, along with my three-inch notebook with all documentation, including the abusive email.

The memo from Christopher detailing my job termination confused Stephanie. In her words, "This has not been approved by this office." She immediately exited the room to check with her other colleagues in case there was an approval of which she was not aware. Stephanie returned to the room with a stressed look on her face. "This memo stating your termination contains false information," she said. "The information in this memo has not been approved." Stephanie told me there was no record of Jackson contacting HR and Christopher Rhodes was obviously given false information about the mutual agreement of termination from the Donor Club with the bogus date of May 31, 2007.

Not only was the information falsified but it was discovered two years later the memo was created by Jackson on his computer.

I was speechless. I was not sure what this all meant but I knew it was proof positive to Stephanie that my supervisor was out of control. As I opened my notebook, I said to her, "I am done with this whole deal." I turned the page to the degrading email. I had told her about the electronic abuse in the past, but I had never shown her the hard copy until now. Stephanie's eyes swiftly moved through several pages in silence and as she turned each page her face showed an indescribable expression. As she got to Jackson's email her face was transformed to a look of utter shock. She lowered her head to read the electronic message, calmly looked up at me and said, "Oh my, we do have a problem!"

Stephanie then asked me if she could speak to Eugene to update him about Jackson's unapproved job termination and his degrading email. I told her she could speak to anyone on my behalf; however, I was not going to speak with Jackson anymore. The look in his eyes at our last face to face was bone chilling and I refused to put myself in his presence anymore. I had established my boundaries with this man and prayed the university would respect them.

Respect

Be strong with your convictions and be willing to stand your ground
it is all about being true to yourself with a true peace of mind
our challenges can overwhelm us combined with terror and fear
but showing individual respect should always remain clear
A superior should be a leader and be courteous among his peers
but crossing the line in disrespect will be evidently clear

As I wiped tears away from my face Stephanie encouraged me to go home and clear my head. I offered to leave her my notebook for viewing, but she insisted I keep it with me. Stephanie immediately called Eugene and informed him of the situation. Within thirty minutes, both Walter and Jackson were in Stephanie's office discussing the status of my job termination.

Later that night I sent her an email:

From: Woodson, Nancy
Sent: Thursday, February 22, 2007
To: Brown, Stephanie
Cc: Doug
Subject: thank you

Stephanie,
I really appreciate all your support during this very difficult time. I did receive the memo from Christopher Rhodes and I am not responding at this time because I will be waiting for you on how to proceed.
Nancy

Stephanie informed Jackson that HR was never informed of a termination agreement. When she asked him why he lied about it he replied, "I was going to talk to you about it today." He admitted to her that it had not been approved by the Human Resources department. Additionally, he had misrepresented it to Christopher Rhodes. (I never heard what Christopher's response was in regard to his name being attached to a fabricated memorandum containing false information.) Stephanie also asked Jackson about the electronic abuse via email. His response was, "I made a mistake." Jackson had broken university policy.

I called a family friend – who happened to be an attorney to ask his legal opinion. He was floored to hear of the abuse and immediately referred me to a specialist in labor laws. I was not going to pursue legal action, but I did want to know my rights as an employee. I felt it was necessary for me to be informed of harassment laws and employee rights.

I was scared to death to know I was the topic of controversy but at the same time I wanted to be heard. I knew I had the documentation to prove his abuse and felt it necessary to have him stopped. I was in a position to pull the cord, because I had a husband supporting me both emotionally and financially. I knew deep in my heart if I lost my job our family would survive. We would have to make some adjustments in our life style, but I was willing to take the risk on behalf of myself and other women in this situation.

CHAPTER 16
Trust

My faith is being tested with patience and pride
the frustration I am experiencing has me very
somber and often makes me cry
in the quick of the moment God rewards me with love through his care
I trust in his timing for the "opportunities" I will share
all the dramas are shaping me for something special I know
I am just unclear of his plan and why I feel so low
I will place each foot forward and stay focused on my academic goal
while concentrating on my family
and never losing confidence with my tormented soul

THE EVENING WAS LONG AND confusing as I tried to process Jackson's actions in regard to the falsified internal memorandum. I could not believe how he deliberately lied to my face and why the university was letting him get away with this irresponsible behavior. But then again if I was disappointed in anyone, it probably was me. I trusted this man time and time again and what a mistake that was.

Stephanie placed a call to Eugene Dunkas, the Vice Chancellor, immediately following her meeting with Jackson and his superior Walter Phillips. She informed him of Jackson's repeated verbal harassment the belligerent email, the inappropriate language combined with the falsified memo. It was later discovered, Jackson not only supplied the erroneous information, but he document did not come from Christopher Rhode's office as he previous stated. I was surprised to find out that her meeting with Walter and Jackson took place within thirty minutes of my departure from her office and it made me sick to my stomach that so many people were learning about the controversy.

Stephanie's email informing me of her meeting:

From: Brown, Stephanie
Sent: Friday, February 23, 2007
To: Woodson, Nancy
Subject: RE: thank you

Nancy,

I emailed Eugene Dunkas yesterday and received a reply from him last night; he's on the road, but we talked this morning. He then called Walter and asked him to meet with me; Jackson came to see me with Walter. Eugene asked that the three of us discuss how we might meet with you to resolve this issue, and he also asked that Christopher Rhodes be part of the solution.

So, we've moved pretty rapidly. I know you were sensitive to wanting me to deal initially with Eugene, and he fully understood that. I know he anticipates that the collective group can work to meet everyone's needs, and he's keenly aware of the situation in which you find yourself.

Walter, Jackson, you and I will meet if you agree. Walter says he will join us if you feel he can be helpful in the process. While I understand your current level of discomfort with Jackson, we really need to bring him into the mix. While Eugene isn't going to meet with us initially, I anticipate that any solutions at which we arrive will need his blessing.

If this works for you, let me know, and I'll see if we can't find a mutually agreeable time to meet.

-Stephanie

I was appreciative of Stephanie's sensitivity to my situation and her keen insight as to whom to invite to the upcoming meeting. I was disappointed Eugene chose not to get involved, as I held his opinion in high regard. I trusted him because he was instrumental in my relocation and he was a fair and ethical person. I anticipated he would defend my position.

Stephanie encouraged me to relax and enjoy the weekend. She was aware of my anxiety and insightful in counseling me about how to discuss the details of Jackson's behavior with the higher ups. We agreed to place the dispute on hold for the weekend and follow up with a conversation on Monday morning. I headed home after our discussion relieved that the week was over but feeling low and defeated due to what lay ahead. I was panicked about the potential repercussions from the week's activities and not quite sure if my supervisors would treat me fairly. I knew Jackson had gone too far and I hoped things would get better, but instead my notebook was growing thicker by the day.

Monday morning came and as promised I received an email from Stephanie requesting a meeting. She was persistent in getting the group together and with each suggestion I was becoming aware of the university's concern with the legal ramifications.

From: Brown, Stephanie
Sent: Monday, February 26, 2007
To: Woodson, Nancy
Subject: Telephone Conversation Friday

Nancy,
If I remember correctly, when we talked Friday afternoon we agreed that I'd wait to hear from you before I initiated the meeting with Christopher, Jackson, Walter, you, and me. I'm not pushing you, but I just wanted to make sure I wasn't supposed to be doing something proactive on this.
Hope you had a great weekend.
Stephanie

Later in the week Jay was scheduled to have his knee scoped, the timing seemed perfect. I had requested time off to care for him during his recovery and the break from the office was a welcome reprieve. Stephanie made several attempts to set up a meeting with the "boys", but I politely declined. I refused to be in the same room with Jackson much less to be cornered into excusing his behavior. It was clear to me from her email that she respected the boundaries I was setting for myself and was respectful of the gravity of my situation.

From: Woodson, Nancy
Sent: Monday, February 26, 2007
To: Brown, Stephanie
Subject: RE: Telephone Conversation Friday

Thank you for following up.
Yes, about the meeting can I get back to you on when? My son Jay
is having knee surgery today and I am leaving for the hospital after
class.
Nancy

Stephanie continued with her attempt to schedule a meeting with
Christopher, Walter, Jackson, and herself. I felt sitting down with the
group of men was not the right thing for me to do. I had gone through
the proper channels. I followed the chain of command and I truly felt
the system had failed me. Had I agreed to participate in the meeting,
I would have been forced to defend myself and my word all over again.
I was not at all interested in attending the kangaroo court. My details
were factual, documented for accuracy, and witnessed by many. I was
done with the madness. "It's Business." All I had wanted was to do my
job, continue my education (requested by the university), and go home
to my family at the end of the day. I had much to be thankful for.

From: Brown, Stephanie
Sent: Monday, February 26, 2007
To: Woodson, Nancy
Subject: RE: Telephone Conversation Friday

I don't want to move on this until you're ready.
Take care of Jay.
-Stephanie

I returned to work two days later and found myself dreading the
impending drama. I sent Stephanie an email informing her I was back
in the office.

From: Woodson, Nancy
Sent: Wednesday, February 28, 2007
To: Brown, Stephanie
Subject: RE: Telephone Conversation Friday

I am in the office today.
Nancy

The meeting was going to have to take place. The questions were when and who would be present? I was not comfortable with Jackson being at the meeting because having him in the room made my skin crawl. I will always remember his bone-chilling deep stare just before he handed me the internal newsletter and falsified memo. I decided to suggest only Christopher Rhodes be present.

From: Brown, Stephanie
Sent: Wednesday, February 28, 2007
To: Woodson, Nancy
Subject: RE: Telephone Conversation Friday
Do you want me to go ahead and arrange the meeting?
-Stephanie

Woodson, Nancy
Sent: Wednesday, February 28, 2007
To: Brown, Stephanie

Subject: RE: Telephone Conversation Friday
How about you and I just meet with Christopher Rhodes?
-Nancy

I was ready to start the process with the meeting. I felt the fewer people present, the quicker we could get to a solution.

From: Brown, Stephanie
Sent: Wednesday, February 28, 2007
To: Woodson

Nancy,
I know that Eugene wanted us all to meet together, but if you, and Christopher and I met, what do we want to try to accomplish? As I understand it, Christopher doesn't have any openings right now.
-Stephanie

According to Stephanie's email, Christopher sounded like he didn't think he should be involved or perhaps he felt like this situation didn't require his immediate attention. I trusted Christopher as much as I trusted Eugene. However, it was very disappointing that he didn't consider this situation to be high on his list of "to do's." I began to realize that having Christopher present might not prove to be the most beneficial for me or add much support to my case.

From: Woodson, Nancy
Sent: Thursday, March 01, 2007
To: Brown, Stephanie
Subject: Thursday

Stephanie,
In a perfect world....you and I would meet with Eugene. The bottom line is I trust Eugene and Christopher has not been part of this process. The memo from Christopher demonstrated to me the one-sidedness of this whole big mess and frankly the thought of a big meeting and feeling like I need to defend myself is not my desire! I am anxious for a solution to this very difficult situation and I am asking for Jackson not to be included from this point forward. I know Eugene doesn't want to be included on the first round but I think involving him from the start would be a great time saver for everyone!
Thank you for all your help!
Nancy

I asked Stephanie if the Chancellor of the university had been informed of the actions of his rogue employee and she responded "Yes, he is aware of the situation." This validated my suspicion of their concerns that my complaint might become a legal matter.

From: Brown, Stephanie
Sent: Thursday, March 01, 2007
To: Woodson, Nancy
Subject: RE: Thursday

With your permission, I will forward this to Eugene. I feel that for both of us to be credible in this process, we need Eugene's permission to exclude Jackson. I understand your position, but I don't want to go over Eugene's head.

I want to make sure I understand exactly the parties you want included in the first meeting: Eugene Dunkas, Stephanie Brown, and Nancy Woodson? And you would like Eugene included but understand he may choose not to do this?

As the weeks passed by, I continued to be an actress in the office. I was in a stressful work environment, but determined not to quit my job or give up on my education. Stephanie was keeping steady pressure on the Vice Chancellor to indentify a new position, but until a position was made available, there was little to report. She was very attentive regarding the lines of communication between all parties. I trusted her completely, as I felt she was my strongest advocate.

From: Woodson, Nancy
Sent: Thursday, March 01, 2007
To: Brown, Stephanie
Subject: RE: Thursday

Yes, you have my permission to forward these emails. My main purpose is to find a solution, not focus on the problem (Jackson)....I want to move forward in a positive way. If Eugene wants Christopher there... that would be fine. The three of us or the four of us...I trust Eugene's authority and will respect his direction!
Thank you!
-N

The stress of this continual process was starting to take a toll on my emotional health. Stephanie could sense I was nearing my breaking point after now an eighteen-month stretch of controversy. She was very considerate and she checked on me regularly. I convinced her I was fine to work in my current position because I knew my patience would pay off with the "perfect" position.

From: Brown, Stephanie
Sent: Thursday, March 01, 2007
To: Woodson, Nancy
Subject: RE: Thursday

I've forwarded your emails to Eugene, and I'll let you know when he responds.

Days turned into weeks and weeks turned into months. The constant worry about my job future and Eugene's lack of time to address the situation was starting to wear on me. I was tired of playing the part of the cheerful staff member. After three months of acting I was worn down and felt like a prisoner in my own office. I sensed freedom was near believing my time in this position was limited. I ask myself, "Just how long will they make me stay in this hell hole?" I continued to do my job and dodging Jackson had become a refined skill. It was exhausting trying to avoid him.

My husband, Doug, was a wonderful support system. He encouraged me to stay focused on the task at hand and not let my emotions interfere with my true objectives:

- Exiting the abusive environment
- Continuing my employment at the university
- Maintaining my benefits
- Continuing my education

Stephanie was busy negotiating with a meeting time and place. She was protective of my wishes while maintaining professionalism. She was protecting both the university and me. "Jackson will fall on his own sword one day," Stephanie said to me. She knew my rights as an employee had been violated and disregarded.

> *I could feel myself lying on the heated ground with blood running down my body. The sweat was dripping into my eyes, as a foggy state was taking over my vision. I could hear the crowds screaming in the distance as their mumbling sounds started to fade in my consciousness. All of a sudden I regained my composure and placed my left hand under my shoulder to help lift my injured body. I was feeling my strength to stand and continue the race. As I stood in an upright but bent position, I felt my limp arm dangling to my side. Not sure of the injury of the motionless limb, I planted my feet and started to head towards the finish line. I was moving forward toward the white line. I knew I was never to look back.*

Through all the stress and drama I realized it was time for me to pause and redirect my focus to my upcoming cancer scan scheduled for April 5th. When suddenly, I thought of a short-term solution:

From: Woodson, Nancy
Sent: Thursday, March 22, 2007
To: Brown, Stephanie
Subject: question

Stephanie,
I just received a message from Eugene Dunkas and he will not be here

tomorrow and is still working on options. What are your thoughts about my taking administrative leave for a couple of weeks....starting Monday 26th – April 9th? I am scheduled for my thyroid and full body scan on Friday, April 5th, which includes an injection Monday and Tuesday (4/2 & 4/3)....a hospital visit for oral medicine on 4/4 and then I have an orthopedic appt. on 4/4...... then go in the tunnel on 4/5 (Good Friday). I think it would benefit me tremendously to be out of this environment. I'm exhausted from dodging people and playing the actress. This whole thing is wearing me out!
Nancy

From: Brown, Stephanie
Sent: Thursday, March 22, 2007
To: Woodson, Nancy
Subject: RE: question

I know Eugene' intention is to meet on Monday or Tuesday. I'm sure that will happen...for one thing, he knows I'll be in the office on Monday and Tuesday and then out the rest of the week.

Administrative leave is something you'd have to request, and it may be a good idea at some point...but I think it would be good for you to be available for the discussion with Eugene.

I suggested this aggressive move for my sanity. There was just too much coming towards me and I knew I needed a break. I had to get out of there.

The next day I picked up the phone in my office and I heard Stephanie's speak a few surprising words. She firmly stated: "Pack up your things and walk out of the office; you are on administrative leave for two weeks with pay from this moment on." "I don't understand," I replied. Stephanie explained that Eugene was not sure where I should be placed so to take the pressure off everyone they decided it best to removing me from hostile work environment while contemplating a potential long-term solution.

"Eugene is working on your new position," she said, "but he needs more time." This will enable you to complete your scan, and when that is behind you, you will be ready to speak with Eugene." I felt so relieved. I was prepared to multi-task with the two situations but thankful I would not have to battle the scan and Jackson together. I was not sure what all this meant for my future at the university, but I was happy to be leaving.

I immediately grabbed several shopping bags in my desk drawer and stuffed all my possessions in them. It was the fastest move ever. I walked into my colleague's office next door and told only her of my immediate departure. With few details communicated, I shared with her that it was the right thing to do and I needed to leave immediately. I remember her words vividly: "You have to do what you need to do." I felt guilty for not saying goodbye to my friends/colleagues in the office before exiting the building, but I had decided the less said the better. I felt such sadness as I drove off the campus; I couldn't believe this was happening. I was starting to see a small ray of hope in what I felt to be a never-ending nightmare.

I called Doug on the way home and explained the radical and sudden change in my work status. He frantically asked me if I had received anything in writing, and I panicked for fear I had not followed proper procedure. I immediately called Stephanie to explain our immediate concerns, and I requested a written statement for my file. She understood my apprehension as she offered to write an official HR statement describing my current administrative leave.

From: Brown, Stephanie
Sent: Friday, March 23, 2007
To: Dunkas, Eugene
Cc: Phillips, Walter; Hyde, Jackson; Woodson, Nancy
Subject: Nancy Woodson's Leave

Eugene,
I talked with Nancy after our conversation this morning, and she agreed that a two-week hiatus to deal with health issues would be beneficial. I explained that you had approved a paid leave for this purpose and that you, she, and I would regroup on April 9 to discuss job options.
There may be some confusion regarding Nancy's status because she did remove her personal items from her office. I reiterated that she has not quit her job nor has the University removed her from it; we are simply taking a two-week breathing spell.
Stephanie

I was gone and so relieved. The weight of the world had been lifted from my shoulders. Now I was able to focus on my next hurdle - my cancer scan.

CHAPTER 17
Baby Steps

I WAS SO RELIEVED TO WALK in my door and announce to my children that I was beginning a two-week hiatus. For the first time, we all felt as if my employer were taking seriously the abusive behavior I had been dealing with for so long. I knew the university was aware Jackson had broken laws. It was now clear to them I would no longer allow myself to be on the receiving end of this man's blatant abuse. Male or female, the inappropriate language and demands were offensive and should never be tolerated in any situation. However, they were protecting Jackson in order to protect themselves. I personally found the university's lack of action disheartening. There is zero tolerance of sexual harassment in the workplace, but the law does not require a zero tolerance for bullying in the work environment.

I reminded myself to break it all down into "Baby Steps" and to take "One Day at a Time." I knew Stephanie was taking care of me and I also knew I had the documentation to prove Jackson's abuse. It was a brilliant move by the university to allow me the time to regain my thoughts and composure.

Baby Steps

We learn them as a baby
and are cheered by others when we fall
it continues as a learning process
with encouragement from all
our journey is revealed time and time again

we often live in determination
until the bitter end
I often tell myself to slow things down and take them as they come
break my challenges down to "Baby Steps"
and stay away from the whole sum
take each day freely with a clear and open mind
try not to get hung up on the little things that often make us unkind

With the two weeks off and my nervous energy kicking in, I decided to take on a new "Martha Stewart" home project. I was tired of looking at our old pine four-poster bed of twenty years and thought revitalizing it would be a wonderful way to keep my mind distracted from all the work drama and my upcoming scan.

The truth is the yearly cancer scan always rattles my cage. Just the physical maintenance as a cancer survivor alone is mentally exhausting and financially draining. I knew deep in my heart that God was steering my ship. Too many things had come together in my family's life: working for a university without a college degree, diagnosed with cancer after only eight months under the university's health plan, being offered a second chance to complete my college degree and receiving tuition benefit. God was so gracious to our family. He was laying the foundation for success. It was now our responsibility to take the gifts he had provided and approach them with hard work and determination. I trusted his guidance and was so thankful for His hand in my life. It may sound strange, but I deeply believe my cancer was a gift from Him. My cancer gave me an indescribable confidence. I found myself no longer scared of failing because my disease reminded me of the limited time we have on this earth. It was time to embrace my passions and be totally in the moment. Cancer empowered me at this time in my life. In many ways, cancer had given a license to be crazy "er" and I was no longer going to wait on things I had put off in my life. There were so many things I wanted to do and try. In the past, I never saw myself good enough to try. I worried that others would make fun of my effort and me. However, over the previous few months of boldly standing up for myself, I finally understood the phrase: "It is better to have tried and failed than never to have tried at all." That statement had become my personal mantra. My cancer had a purpose. It gave me strength and confidence to embrace my life.

Doug was not in favor of my disassembling our bed of twenty-one years. In fact, he gave me strict orders not to touch the piece of furniture. I struggled with his command for about thirty minutes, while I was heading to the neighborhood store for supplies and wood stain. I called a contractor who owed a chain saw and asked him to hesitantly cut off the four-foot columns of the bed. In spite of Doug's objections, I could envision a new life for the dated piece, and felt certain he would approve of the finished product. When it came to Doug and decorating, it was always easier to ask for forgiveness than permission. I loved transforming something old and tired into something fresh and new. It was a cheaper way to update and required only my time, labor and a few dollars.

As the contractor carefully placed the powerful saw on the wood, I let out a sigh. I found it difficult to witness the mutilation of the bed, so I quietly exited the room. When he shut off his saw, I quickly returned to the room to find the old, tired bed taking on a new identity with a modern décor. I was feeling more confident about my decision, but was anxious about Doug's returning to the chaotic home. I pondered all day how I would gently break the news to him that he would be sleeping on the couch.

Doug casually walked in through the back door from a long grueling workday to find his bed disassembled and lying in multiple pieces. I assured him my new project would not last long and he would be returning to his bed within a few nights. I didn't realize the combination of oil based paint and high humidity would result in almost two weeks of drying time. Oops. What started as a few nights on the couch turned into two weeks of a huge inconvenience. It was a small problem for the logistics of my family's sleeping arrangements, but the timing was right for him to be sweet and understanding with his wife since she would soon be undergoing her annual cancer scan.

When the bed was drying I would jump in my car and return to our old neighborhood looking at houses. Suddenly, I spotted what I thought was my "dream" house with a new "for sale" sign in their front yard. I immediately called Doug and his response surprised me. "I would love to move back to the hood, sell our house first." We toured the newly listed house three times with our realtor Kelly and within a few days the "for sale" sign was placed in our yard.

The weeklong preparation and subsequent scan revealed no return of the cancerous cells to the thyroid bed. I felt relieved to have this "hurdle" crossed off my list and thrilled to have my newly designed bed finally completed. The two weeks were productive and mentally rejuvenating for my soul. I felt confident Eugene would find the right position for me within his department. I was just so thankful I didn't have to be an actress anymore. I was anxious about the upcoming meeting about my relocation. Doug could feel my anxiety and he did something that both surprised and encouraged me. He sent me this email:

From: Woodson, Doug
Sent: Wednesday, March 27, 2007
To: Woodson, Nancy
Subject: RE: Discussion with Eugene

A few thoughts for you to consider for your meeting:

1) Whatever time Stephanie and Eugene set for the meeting, agree to it, even if you have to miss class or reschedule an appointment...
2) Keep in mind that even though you are the only one who has been wronged, this situation has placed immense pressure and stress on Eugene and Walter...
3) Continue to not discuss this with anyone ...
4) Continue to read Joel's daily devotional (and forward to me)...
5) When the offer is made don't feel like you have to give them an immediate response...
6) Be Ms Puppy, the positive person that everyone we know wants to be around...

Please read this carefully, print it out for your notebook and delete from your computer...

Doug

I loved this message and read it again and again. No, I did not delete it from my computer because I needed it as a reminder to stay positive and keep my eye on the main objective.....to keep my job.

I returned to campus with a small spring in my step. I looked forward to hearing Eugene thoughts regarding my new position on campus. The meeting would take place in his conference room with only Stephanie present. I feared colleagues would see me and ask about my two-week disappearance. I also was nervous that I would reveal my emotions if I was disappointed with his suggestion, so I began to silently coach myself not to react positively or negatively to his proposal.

Eugene stated what he considered to be the right fit for me with details of the newly created position. I considered this new job location to be a wonderful opportunity. Contrary to my husband's advice to carefully consider any offer made, I immediately accepted his recommendation.

The new job offered me the means to be successful with the university, my family and my schoolwork. So much for discussing it with Doug... it was a wonderful opportunity.

After the meeting, Stephanie and I remained in the conference room where I thanked her sincerely for standing up for me and my education. Because of this woman, I had challenged my abuser and remained an employee the university.

Within two months of my departure from Jackson's tyrannical and abusive rule, two of the three staff members resigned from their positions. One moved out of state and the other accepted another job on campus because of the harassing treatment she had received from Jackson Hyde too. I'd like to think in some small way my actions paved the way and gave others the courage to stand up for themselves. The truth was no one knew what happen, they only speculated.

Chapter 18

Green Socks

MY NEW POSITION WITH THE university started within the week. This new job was all I had hoped it would be with my new team and six weeks of training. Part of the training included accompanying my new boss to Houston to make personal introductions to alumni with whom I had worked with in previous years. Another business trip to Houston was somewhat unsettling given my past history.

The contract to sell our house was finalized so now it was time to submit a contract on my future dream house. I was so excited to finally make an offer. Doug was trying hard to find the time to draw up the contract on the new house deal.

I was on the road with my new boss, Richard Deen, enjoying the scenic drive when suddenly, I sensed the need to call and check in with my older sister, Terry. Even though Terry was six years older we had always had a close bond between the two of us. My sister had one of the kindest hearts I have ever known. She lived for her family and her children were her focus. When she was not taking care of her family she was either cooking or tending to her huge vegetable garden in her manicured yard. She had recently become an "empty nester" and was finding it very difficult to be alone. As the years moved along she was finding herself alone. She had become a prisoner in her own home. Her husband, Dudley, had always worked long hours in the furniture business and now her kids were grown and gone. Her trepidation increased and she began drinking during the day to numb her sadness and loneliness. Her casual drink or two became several on regular basis ultimately led to her destruction.

I knew deep down inside that her drinking had become a problem but what was ahead for her and our family was something I never could have imagined.

I made the call during mid morning or better known as the "coffee talk" hour. I immediately noticed a slur in her speech. I have always been able to detect when someone had been drinking, as I would refer to it as having the "gift." I had recently called her on her destructive behavior, but it only infuriated her and made her defensive. My attempts to address her destructive behavior brought stress to our relationship and with limited support from other family members. I eventually lessened my efforts. Over the last six months of her life our regular daily phone calls became less frequent. She fabricated an excuse for everything. It didn't matter if it was just an informal family get together or a major holiday; there was always a reason she could not come. She developed anxiety about leaving her home, another sign of her abusive drinking that we didn't pick up on. It was saddening to witness her self-destruction, but I found that not confronting her dysfunction became a coping mechanism for us all.

As I hung up the phone during the drive to Houston I was not sure of what action to take. Richard was surprised by the family drama as he heard much of the conversation. I found myself choosing my words carefully with my family members when talking about Terry. I immediately called my younger sister, Kristen, and asked her to call Terry to evaluate the situation to confirm my suspicion. I wasn't sure what I would do with the information except perhaps, tattle to my mother which had not proven to be very effective in the past.

Terry stopped taking phone calls and I never imagined that my early morning call would be her last. When Kristen didn't reach her she called our brother-in-law and without hesitation he informed her of Terry's grim condition. He believed Terry's liver was failing and her body was shutting down. He stated he had offered to take her to the emergency room several times, but she strongly declined each time. He described her as "sitting on the couch in a deep stare" and with the passing of every hour she slowly slipped into a semi-conscious state.

Kristen called me back in a panic, and we immediately decided to let our mother know what was going on. The conversations were building from city to city. Within hours my brother's wife decided to make the four-hour drive from Oklahoma City to Terry's home to assess the situation. Terry didn't answer the continuous phone calls and I couldn't help but imagine her sitting in her dark living room slipping into a deep despair. The mental images were heartbreaking as I visualized her body slowly shutting down. My deepest pain came from believing she was traveling this frightful and painful journey alone.

Terry's husband, Dudley, returned home several times to check on her throughout the day. In the early afternoon he entered the house and Terry slowly stood up then lost consciousness and crashed to the floor. As she fell her head struck the coffee table. As he helped her back onto the couch her shirt lifted and Dudley saw her abnormally swollen stomach. He frantically dialed 911 and within a few minutes the paramedics arrived and confirmed his worst fear: "Sir, your wife is having liver failure."

How had Terry fallen this far? How could a mother, wife, daughter, sister, and friend to so many be dying before our eyes in this manner? How did this happen? When Kristen called me back and said, "Terry is in liver failure," I was in shock.

My boss and I had reached our destination, and once again I put on my acting hat as we called on donors. As the day wore on I felt more and more apprehensive because I didn't have my own transportation so I couldn't return home. My sister was on the brink of death and I was 300 miles away. Feeling helpless I immediately called Doug to give him the news and he went to the hospital to assess the situation.

While trying to make sense of this situation I received a phone call that added more weight to the already profound burden on my heart and mind. My real estate agent called to inform me of two other offers coming in on my dream house. I was so overwhelmed. I just couldn't process everything at once. I took a deep breath, planted my feet, and recited two of my favorite phrases "Baby Steps" and "It's Business." I called Doug as he drove to the hospital and informed him of the troubling house news. I asked him to prepare a contract so we could submit our offer the next day. Time was of the essence, and I didn't want to lose this house and potentially be forced to rent again.

Doug entered the hospital ER and was directed to Terry's room. He was immediately taken aback by her appearance. Terry's prognosis was grim, and according to my husband her condition was deteriorating.

He later said that his first view of Terry's semi-conscious, lifeless body was devastating to witness. He described her as unrecognizable and her bulging eyes were beet red, swollen and oozing with infection. Her stomach was twice normal size and she was connected to multiple IV's. Her arms and legs were tied down to the bed to keep her from pulling out the tubes. She drifted in and out of consciousness and each time she woke up she tried hard to get up so they harnessed her to the bed. Doug was filled with emotion. Overcome by the attending physician's blunt statement, Doug had to go outside to gather his composure. Upon re-entering the ER he didn't tell Dudley what he had learned or anyone until two weeks later. Terry's liver had shut down and her existence was now hour to hour. At one point Doug became angered by the lack of attention Terry was getting so he approached the ER doctor behind the nurse's station and was quickly told to calm down because there was "nothing they could do." Doug was in unfamiliar territory and since the doctor and nurses didn't give any information he decided to get some information on his own. He called a physician friend late that night from the hospital, described Terry's symptoms and condition and was told that it sounded like the damage was done and chances for survival slim.

By the time Richard and I had finished our afternoon appointments that early evening taking a flight back was not an option. I requested we leave as soon as possible the next morning following our two early meetings the following day.

I couldn't believe I felt like a hostage in a five-star hotel. I spent most of the night on the phone with family members and badgering Doug to write up the offer for the house. He promised me he would get it done the next day.

Due to my anxiousness Richard couldn't drive fast enough. I wished his car was an exact replica of "Chitty Chitty Bang Bang," the car that lifted into the air, soaring over everything and getting to its destination faster. Instead, I peered out the window worrying about my sister as he crawled down the highway.

When I finally arrived home, I immediately drove to the hospital as I continued to receive updates from Doug. He carefully prepared me for what I was about to see. As I stepped off of the elevator my mother and father greeted me. My mother was devastated. Her daughter was dying, but the most upsetting piece of the unsolved puzzle was why had she done this to herself? What causes someone to abuse themselves to this extent, and why didn't she ever reach out to anyone to reveal her pain? She had to know she was ill and the damage she had done to her body.

I entered Terry's room and saw my dying sister. In an instant, love and compassion overwhelmed me. I did not have feelings of anger for her harming her body, but of unconditional love. I was overcome by her appearance and condition and I could feel my family's love throughout the room. My sister was truly devoted to my mother and I am convinced she did not intentionally bring about her premature illness. Her poor decisions however, would have lasting consequences on her and her family.

With family members coming in and out of town, my home became a bed and breakfast during the crisis. I extended an open invitation to family as long as everyone pitched in, took out the trash, walked the dogs, and emptied the dishwasher.

Our contract on my dream house was in competition with others. We felt like we had a good chance because we knew the sellers. The stress of selling our house combined with Terry's condition and the competition for the new house was starting to take its toll on us. Two days later I received the devastating rejection from our real estate agent regarding the seller's decision to go with another contract for their house. I can remember to this day where I was standing in the hospital hall when she gave me the disappointing news. "The buyers rejected your contract," she stated. I grabbed the handicap railing along the sides of the hall and felt my knees buckle. "What are you telling me, she rejected our contract, and we have nowhere to move? Did you tell her my sister is dying? They know us, what the hell? Call her back and offer more money. We have to have somewhere to go," I pleaded with her. "The deal is dead," she firmly stated. "They sold it to their neighbor." Within in seconds, my world came crashing down again and my world went dark. Terry was dying; I had to pack up my house and once again and had nowhere to go.

Jay's graduation from high school was right around the corner. A multitude of parties and other obligations were in front of us. I constantly reminded myself to remain calm and break my responsibilities down into "Baby Steps." Jay was thrilled to be ending his high school career, but the celebration was compromised by his dying aunt. Emotions were running high with everyone. It was my job to steer the ship out of the "perfect storm" and into calmer waters.

Hours turned into days and days turned into weeks. It was difficult to spend so many hours in the hospital sitting next to my dying sister. Walking to the crushed ice machine down the hall became my favorite past time as I found myself peeking in everyone's room out of curiosity. What a creeper I had become out of boredom.

Terry was never one who enjoyed my favorite passions - spa treatments. In fact, she hated to be touched and would always refuse any type of pampering. When one day, I came up with a creative way to spend my time with her, as I turned her hospital room into a massage room. I entered her room one morning to find her husband Dudley standing by her bed. Even though she was fading in and out of consciousness, we knew she could hear our conversation. I excitedly shared with Dudley my new idea of a daily massage for Terry. He quickly reminded me of her dislike for the treatment. I laughed and told him, "She can tell me to stop when she can make me."

Terry was connected to multiple machines and the beeping of the ventilator informed us of each breath. As I started to massage her hot body, each stroke was a way for me to express my love. With each rub I could feel myself gaining strength while transferring my love. Dudley stood there in amazement as her blood pressure fell and her breathing eased. "She likes it," he remarked, "who would think?" I moved to the end of the bed and uncovered her limp feet. I rubbed lotion into my hands and delivered my energy to her through a foot massage. For a person who really doesn't like feet giving the gift of a foot massage was a stretch.

With each stroke I could visualize the mental image of Mary and Elizabeth rubbing Jesus' feet in my mind. I could tell by her dropping blood pressure that she was enjoying the treatment as I placed a pair of green socks on her feet. The socks were a cabbage green color and the bright rainbow color added a new dynamic to the room. The experience reminded me of the many manicures I had organized at the local children's hospital with Bailey and a small group of her friends. It also reminded me of a community service outing Bailey and I had participated in at the Union Gospel Mission giving manicures and pedicures to the homeless. I knew how stimulating the gift of touch can be to a person and that compelled me to honor my sister this way. Terry was relaxed and serene after the treatment and each person entered the room, she lifted her feet to show off her new green socks. As she lay dying in her hospital bed she was communicating her heartfelt love for her family. She knew we were all there, she knew we loved her, and she knew we wanted her to pull out of this irreversible condition. The massage time became our daily ritual. It was our special time together until she re-entered ICU.

Doug was scheduled to attend an annual convention in Las Vegas, and frankly having of one less body in the house was starting to sound appealing. I encouraged him to go on the five-day trip knowing a break from the stressful "house of crisis" would recharge his mental state and simplify my routine.

The very thought of looking for another house was exhausting. The tediousness of scouring at the newspaper for multiple properties required more energy than my mind could handle. My sister was dying and I had sixty days to find a new house. I was completely overwhelmed with this task under the current circumstances.

The house was pretty quiet over the weekend as mother and dad returned home to Oklahoma City for a few days of solitude. My realtor, Kelly called a few days later to encourage me to tour a list of properties she had generated. With a few hours to kill on a Sunday afternoon before heading to the hospital I decided to take her advice to view the seven new properties. The first four houses were of zero interest and my lack of desire rapidly declined. Feeling unmotivated to complete the tour the fifth house was an unexpected surprise.

Kelly and I entered the house and instantly it felt like my new home. "This is it," I replied. "I want this house, let's write it up." With a look of confusion on her face she said, "Don't you want Doug to see it first?" "He will, but this house is perfect for our family. I want to make an offer today, I can't risk losing another house and my time is too limited." Not really sure how to pitch the new house to my husband who was nine hundred miles away over the phone, I nonetheless dialed his cell phone in a confident tone. "I found THE house." For the first time in weeks Doug heard a positive lift in my voice. "Great news," he said. "I am looking forward to seeing it when I get home." I replied, "We don't have four days to wait, we really need to move on this house today." There was a long silence on the other end of the phone. Unlike me, my husband is methodical, likes to analyze and contemplate. We didn't have time for that. I could sense Doug's thought process. Is my wife losing her mind? "What are they asking for the house and what do you want to offer?" "Don't worry," I replied," I have it all under control." Doug consented to me submitting a contract provided the offer could be terminated within 24 hours of him seeing the house. So we compromised and agreed on an amount to offer.

After a couple counters Doug returned and we had the property under contract. As soon as he saw it he immediately fell in love with our new home. "Well done," he excitedly stated, "You were right, this house if perfect for us." God's timing was perfect. Considering another contract came in at the same time as ours and the buyer chose ours something positive happened to our family.

As the week wore on Terry's condition stabilized. Recovery was becoming a possibility according to the doctor. With her improvement the out-of-town family members decided it was time to return home on a Friday afternoon we all gathered in Terry's room and said our goodbyes. With everyone around her bed my two younger sisters kissed her on the cheek with tears in their eyes. I vividly remember mother rubbing her limp hands because she was anxious about leaving her oldest daughter.

Doug and I encouraged my parents that it was a good time to head home for a few days as we promised to update them daily. Mother needed the break so the time was right for her to leave. She needed to sleep in her own bed and remove herself from the stress-filled environment to recharge her battery. I walked my parents and sister to the parking lot to say goodbyes, because we were all feeling confident her health was starting to turn around and it was a safe time for them to return to their homes. I walked back into Terry's room and whispered in her ear that mother would be back to see her in three days. With a dark look in her eyes she slowly lifted her head and mumbled three days is too long. I was perplexed by her comment and realized at that moment, she knew she was dying and didn't want her mother to leave her side. I stayed with Terry throughout the day as the next morning she had rapidly declined and they moved her back to the ICU.

Terry's daughter, Cary and I entered a quiet hospital on that lonely Memorial Day Monday. As we entered the ICU area, the halls were vacant and eerily silent. Terry's room was dark and warm as her frail body lay somberly alone in a comatose state. The antiseptic smell of the hospital with the light yet distinctive beeping sounds of the life saving machines will be forever etched in my memory. To this day I hear those sounds.

Cary and I approached her bedside as we ignored the presence of the many tubes protruding from her feeble body. My sister's body was failing again; her existence sustained only by electricity and technology. Sweet Cary was suddenly overcome with emotion as she laid her body on top of her mother's chest and sobbed. She knew her mother would never return to her as she struggled to feel her remaining breaths. It was in that exact moment we both knew she was never coming back to us. The moment was surreal as it dawned on me that Terry would never see Cary walk down the aisle or hold her grandchildren. Cary was completely broken and devastated. I found myself in a place I'd never been before. There were few words to say.

Being raised in the Catholic Church I felt the time had come to ask for "last rites." Terry was a spiritual person, but her faith was of a personal nature. She did not embrace the many opportunities of organized religion and was intimidated by public worship. However, I knew the importance of completing the sacraments with my mother and was compelled to honor her unspoken wishes. I asked a nurse for a Catholic priest and she informed me he was in the room next door. Father Hall entered the room, and I immediately felt a spiritual connection to this man of God. His compassion and love towards my sister, my niece, and me was breathtaking. It was at that exact moment I realized the time had come. My sister was dying. She was going to receive the sacrament of "last rites," and even though I was devastated, I considered it a privilege to witness this sacred event.

As the priest opened his Bible and began the traditional sacrament, Cary and I cried with an uncontrollable outburst while holding her hands and stroking her body. Within a few seconds of the opening prayer, I looked at my dying sister and noticed her chin shaking with sentiment, and any doubt she felt with her struggling body were now being confirmed. She knew we were there and I know she knew she was receiving the sacrament of last rites. With our tears dripping on her sheets, Father concluded the formal ritual with a genuine deep concern for the two of us. I was spiritually drawn to this man and his loving heart. I knew my mother would feel comfortable with him so I asked if he could be available for Terry's funeral. I couldn't believe those words actually came out of my mouth. She was still alive and I was planning her funeral. It made me feel uneasy, but I knew Terry's death was inevitable so my "It's Business" mentality took over. He accepted our request immediately and graciously. Cary and I slowly regained control of our physical state and said one last goodnight to our Sweet Terry.

Cary and I left the hospital that night in somewhat of a mental fog as we contemplated all the details of my oldest sister's funeral. It was a draining process spiritually, emotionally and physically. I couldn't believe this was truly happening to her and our family. I desperately wanted to fix it for her, but knew I couldn't. I closed my eyes momentarily and visualized her waking up and putting an end to this madness from the last three weeks. But it wasn't going to happen and there was nothing I could do. She was going to die. It was not a question of "if" but "when."

The next day I decided to go into work and make an appearance. I was drained and exhausted, but I knew I must stay strong and live my life. I needed to communicate the circumstances to my new boss. Once I entered his office he calmly told me to do what I needed to do to take care of my family and myself during this difficult time. To this day I vividly remember Richard's kind words and the relief he gave me that day. He was truly amazing.

As I started tackling the stack of work on my desk when all of a sudden, my office phone rang. It was my brother-in-law, Dudley carefully reciting the words he had just received from the doctor: "Machines are keeping Terry alive." They (medical professionals) have exhausted all avenues for survival and recovery and we are at the end of the road. To this day, Dudley's words play over and over in my mind: "It is over." It is time to take her off the machines. I felt so helpless and lost. There was nothing anyone could do, and I came to the realization that I was going to lose my big sister, my friend and the closest companion relative to my youngest daughter, Lawrence. It was really over.

Dudley asked me to handle the difficult task of calling my parents to communicate Terry's fate and discuss the painful yet necessary decision to disconnect the machines. In one way I did not want to be responsible for this part of the process, but on the other hand, someone had to step up and stay strong in addressing this daunting duty and I knew I was the family member best suited to do it so I called my parents immediately.

With a sudden decline, Terry's condition took on a rapid downward spin. With a failing liver, fluid filled lungs, labored breathing, failing kidneys and a suggested tracheotomy, the family came together to make a gut wrenching decision. The end was here and our family was forced to determine Terry's fate. In multiple conversations and a mutual family agreement, it was decided it was time to remove the ventilator and discontinue all medication.

The three of us agreed with her family's request to terminate all life support and I assured my mother this was the "loving" thing to do as we honored her and her memory. Mother sobbed and cried out for her daughter's life. The conversation was full of love and respect and for a brief moment was conducted in full "business mode." This was truly one of the saddest moments of my life.

Dudley, Cary, Doug and I were to be present for the final goodbye. I knew deep in my heart that my sister would not have wanted to continue living in such an awful state. I pulled into the hospital parking lot and spotted my brother Tim in the parking lot who had just traveled from Oklahoma City. We made eye contact and met at the electronic doors.

We started to make our way down the long, sterile smelling hallway as he curiously asked me for condition and amount of improvement. I immediately realized he didn't know how grave her status was nor of her vegetative condition. He was stunned to learn that we were about to disconnect life support and say goodbye; his facial expressions was one of disbelief and hopelessness.

Silence dominated Terry's hospital room except for the incessant beeping and buzzing of the life support system and monitoring equipment, but you could feel a groundswell of passion, sadness, fear and love that had filled the room in respect for my dying sister. One at a time, everyone made their way to her bedside daughter Cary first, then husband Dudley, my brother Tim and me. Doug stayed back in the corner of the room out of respect for the immediate family. Outburst of emotion continually drowned out the machines and once everyone said goodbye we migrated to various places in the room away from the bed. The nurse technician then entered the room making eye contact with each of us and in a business-like fashion pressed two buttons, flipped one switch, removed the ventilator and exited the room without a word. You could have heard a pin drop as we all stood in silence, motionless, as if frozen, waiting and watching the heart monitor. What felt like an eternity probably lasted less than five minutes as the bright, green neon line changed its shape and eventually went flat.

She was gone. Until that moment I had no idea that a person could experience profound sadness and profound honor simultaneously. I had the privilege of being with my sister during her death. It was heart breaking and heartwarming at the same time. I loved my sister and she loved her family. Her children were her life. Tragically, she just didn't know what to do with her life after they grew up.

Sister

my life is full of sadness
I miss her so much
the memory of her green socks stings my heart
but reminds me of her loving touch.
when I remember her unconditional love
I vividly think of her softly saying "goodbye"
I will hold her memory close until
we're reunited in the sky

The out pouring of affection from my colleagues regarding my sister's death was comforting for the emotional forced re-entry. I knew keeping physically active would be beneficial for my sanity. With all the work conflict and now combined with the loss of Terry just getting up in the morning and getting dressed was a challenge. When one day I received the most inspirational email from one of the women I had come to admire and respect in the last two years.

From: Brown, Stephanie
Sent: Thursday, June 14, 2007
To: Woodson, Nancy
Subject: Condolences

Nancy,

I just learned about your sister's death today, and I want you to know how much I grieve for your loss. You have been through so much.

I understand that her death was caused by liver failure and I have become an advocate of organ donations.

Richard says you and his office are a great match. I hope you're enjoying the new arrangement as much as he is.

Stephanie

As I read her email, my heart sank to my feet. I was finally feeling validation for my hard work but most importantly I was feeling strength through her words. I could feel my "mojo" coming back just a little; a small spring in my step was returning......it was one of those life-changing moments. Once again, I was reminded how a simple email with encouragement can change someone's day.

From: Woodson, Nancy
Sent: Thursday, June 14, 2007
To: Brown, Stephanie
Subject: RE: Condolences

You are so sweet. Thank you! This has been the saddest time in my life. I have learned so much about the liver and its function to the body. She was so sick and it came so fast. After the liver failed, she was in the hospital for 2 weeks – ICU for 8 days. Her kidneys failed, along with so many other things.

I am just so grateful I had my job position secured. I could not have dealt with my sister Terry and with the job stress at the same time. I guess God really does know our limits...

I am sorry I have not written you a thank you note, but the time has just flown by. We are moving at the end of June – can you believe that? I haven't packed a box! To think I was a boring housewife just 4 years ago and now having this over the top life really amazes me. I am so thankful for it every day and I have you to thank the most. Thank you for everything that you did for me and for my family. I promise I will make you proud!

Have a wonderful day!

Nancy

Stephanie's response made me smile.

From: Brown, Stephanie
Sent: Thursday, June 14, 2007
To: Woodson, Nancy
Subject: RE: Condolences

So glad you're doing so well. Just one observation...I cannot believe you were ever a boring housewife...or a boring anything.

CHAPTER 19

Hurt

TERRY'S DEATH OVERSHADOWED THE UPCOMING move into our new home as well as the planning for Bailey's debutante season coming up in the fall. Between scheduling appointments for the new house, party planning, family activities, work, and school, my life was at full capacity.

My son, Jay, was excited about his freshman year of college, but with all the drama in our life it didn't hit me that my second child was going to college until a few weeks before his departure. He was ready to experience his freedom, but for me having him stay in Fort Worth was an emotional safe haven. I considered it the best of both worlds: having both Bailey and Jay close enough when I needed a hug, but far enough away to give them freedom and independence.

As summer approached the move was now my main focus and there was much to do. We all felt good about returning to the side of town we had lived in for twenty years and I knew it would make life easier. It was a bit depressing to think about packing up everything we owned again and having to live out of boxes again, but I knew the end result would be positive for our family. The emotional and psychological pain of Terry's death made it difficult to enjoy everyday life. Moving into a new home that was substantially better than any we had owned should have been a cause for celebration, but it sure didn't feel that way. Each day the sun would rise and give the beautiful gift of light, and I took this as a positive sign to keep moving forward. I had so many things to be thankful for, and yet there was so much to accomplish. My school work kept my mind on a positive track. My mind would often drifted back on my admission's essay as I compared myself to Dorothy heading down the yellow brick road for that college diploma. I feared that if I did not continue walking on the yellow brick road, I would become paralyzed in sadness. My biggest fear was succumbing to grief and depression. This fear motivated me as well. I could feel myself emerging from the grief that had consumed me for weeks as I continued to pursue my goal.

Early evenings were the hardest time for me because Terry and I would talk and discuss our day. Of my seven siblings I was the closest to her. Many times I would pick up the phone and dial her number only to realize she was not there. For awhile I would call her voice mail just to hear her voice. My heart was truly broken and every day I questioned what I could have done to help save my sister. My family realized that we would never know the extent of Terry's emotional and physical pain. There were so many questions and very few answers and only she knew the truth.

Moving back to the familiar side of town would be logistically better for our family especially Lawrence. She was entering sixth grade and the move put her in walking distance to her closest friends and allowed carpooling convenience for her working parents. Every working mother appreciates a little help now and then. I was on overload emotionally and physically, but once again, I told myself to break it down into "Baby Steps" and "Take One Day at a Time." I had the logistics of the move mapped out in my head while maintaining my work regimen. Everything was coming together nicely from a timing standpoint when out of the blue, the real estate closing on our old house was delayed due to our buyer's inability to sell her house in another state. This created a domino effect that brought three transactions to a screeching halt, and with most of possessions in boxes! I was fit to be tied. I was devastated and Doug was frustrated to no end. We found ourselves again in the middle of a highly stressful situation where we had zero control over the solution. In a matter of six weeks I had dealt with my illness, the death of a sister, a child graduating from high school and now a stalled house move. Summer was upon us as was the start of a new fiscal year at work. The start of a fiscal year also brought the opportunity for a pay raise, as I was looking forward to an increase, but upon receiving my electronic pay stub for the month of June I calculated a meager 1.5 percent increase instead of the usual 3 percent plus. I immediately called HR inquiring about the amount anticipating a wrongful calculation. I was told the low percentage raise was based on "merit" system graded out by my previous boss, Jackson Hyde. My immediate suspicion was I was experiencing another form of retaliation by this man, after gathering myself and discussing it with Doug I decided to not challenge the system. Some increase was better than no increase and besides that it felt as if ......my fight was gone......or so I thought at that moment.

I was however, very curious to know Richard's opinion and/or his knowledge of Jackson's revengeful behavior. As I entered Richard's office, I emotionally informed him of Jackson's punitive actions towards me. Richard's response floored me; "Doesn't surprise me because of your personal relationship with him and your departure from his staff." "That was personal," I replied and "This is Business!" Jackson's abuse and retaliation was continuing even after I was no longer under his supervision.

With the first five weeks of summer school coming to a close I reminded myself the importance of staying on course academically, and I needed to sign up for the second session of summer school. I submitted the necessary form for Richard to sign, a prerequisite for my registration to attend class during the day.

When a few days had passed without a response I began to get anxious because classes tend to fill up and I sensed a conflict was brewing over my request. Finally, one day I casually entered Richard's office and requested the signed form only to hear him say, "Eugene wants you to visit with you regarding your class schedule." It was déjà vu with conversations and conflicts about my academic plan. His lack of confidence in his words must have been evident on my face, and he quickly said there was no cause for concern hoping to head off a confrontation. He asked me to email Eugene immediately and to request a meeting as I was thinking to myself; her we go again. Eugene didn't hesitate to responding to my electronic message and asked if Richard and I would come up to his office right away.

As we entered his office, I broke the ice by commenting that it felt like I had been sent to the principal's office. Neither of them appeared amused and Eugene motioned for to take a seat at the conference table and we small talked briefly. Eugene rapidly changed the tone of the conversation stating, "I know we all have a lot going on, so I will get straight to the point." The mood and language was very courteous yet business-like when out of the blue Eugene said. "Nancy, I am very upset with you taking classes during the day and not making the time up, and "frankly, I think you are taking advantage of me and the university." I sat there motionless listening intently to his remarks without comment with a shocking look on my face as his volume increased and his face turned beet red and his body started to shake. I had never seen Eugene like this and it was quite a surprise. He looked like a vein was about to burst in his forehead. "Where is this coming from?" I asked. "We have already addressed this issue; you told me I was allowed to take one class during the day in our last meeting with Stephanie Brown and that I should do whatever I needed to get this done."

He sternly repeated himself, "You have taken advantage of me and this university and everyone is talking about you; everyone is asking "Why does Nancy Woodson get to take time off for classes during the day?" You have put me in a very bad position and from this point on you will not be allowed to take classes during the day." At this point he was shouting again, his body was still shaking, but no broken veins. I was so shocked by the vehemence of his words I was speechless. I was unable to tell him about the many lunches I had at my desk as I kept working and the many evenings I worked past 5:00 o'clock. I didn't get the chance to communicate the multiple trips I took with Richard on appointments in Dallas, many lasted into the evening. My supervisor's incessant demand of "making up the time" was always a nebulous thing. They never defined how they expected me to do this nor did they take into account all the times I worked after hours. Doug often consoled me about this by pointing out micro-managing employees does not work. I was so taken aback by his anger combined with the emotional and physical exhaustion, my mind felt as if it was moving in slow motion. Eugene is a calm, quiet type of person who rarely shows emotion so it caused me to wonder why he got so worked up. I suspected a fellow employee was envious of my agreement had gone to him getting him so worked up.

I could not believe I was experiencing more harassment by yet another person and that the school issue was being raised again. I was slow to react to his emotional outburst, it was not just about the nature of the conversation but the way he was communicating it to me. I stood firmly up to this man as I yelled with disbelief, "I can't believe you think I have taken advantage of you. That breaks my heart and I can't believe the way you are yelling at me." I was overcome with emotion and I burst into tears. I don't think the floodgates broke because Eugene was yelling at me so much, as all the emotions and stress had built up inside of me and at the exact moment released. My house was packed up for a move that might not happen and the thought of unpacking to stay in my existing house was starting to push me over the edge. The stress of Eugene's tirade was causing me to crash. I could feel I was going down.

I was in a forward position, moving towards the white line. I was embarrassed at the fall and within a few second, I could feel a painful twinge radiating down my right arm. The exhaustion was starting to take over my body and with each step I was carefully placing one foot in front of the other. I was starting to feel a loss of balance while starting to doubt my ability to lift my injured body over the continuous wooden obstacles. I was clearly the last one in the race, but I continued to coach myself to keep moving towards the finish line. At this point it was not about winning; it was about finishing what I had started.

Eugene suddenly interrupted having regained his composure and he apologized for his outburst. My tears were flowing as I struggled to catch my breath. I had reached my emotional limit. I sincerely told him I accepted his apology, but my heart was still broken if he really thought I took advantage of him and the university. His comments and allegations indicated that he did not know me at all. I informed him that the school issue was what started the dysfunctional environment on his staff which escalated to disrespect and ultimately harassment. I communicated how I was still upset over how that situation was handled (or not handled) by sweeping it under the rug and not properly notifying the hierarchy of our organization. "As far as everyone talking about me, I haven't heard a thing," I said. In a harsh tone, Eugene replied, "You wouldn't." Richard just sat still in silence.

I was shocked at the meanness and lack of professionalism from this man who held a high position at this well-respected university. I told him I tried not to get involved in office politics because frankly I did not have the time or the energy. I would go into what I refer to as the "tunnel" (my office) and zone out focusing only on my work. I explained to Eugene that my time was limited, but I could handle the office hours through my organizational skills, being able to multi task by planning my day in my head then organizing my thoughts according to the hours in the day. He then asked me specifically what my exact academic schedule was and how much school I had left. I explained the re-evaluation of my transcript and how this new process had enabled the opportunity to graduate faster, but it would require me to take a full consecutive six hours along while at the same time performing my full time work position. I inquired about a ¾ time position and he angrily told me "No." With the campaign gaining strength we would need everyone working hard and no one on his staff would be allowed to work less than full time.

The meeting was very stressful and I found myself taking small gasps of air between wiping away the tears from my face. I didn't handle myself in as professional a manner as I had hoped. The stress and the emotion of this issue overwhelmed me. I told Eugene, "If I can find the extra hours from my class time and in my life, then the university can have them." It was just five weeks ago I lost my sister and I am doing the best I can. I explained our family was moving again which was consuming my time when not at work. "I have children and a household to manage, and frankly I am getting tired of having to explain every part of my life." I asked Eugene why it was looked upon so positively when some employees religiously sat at their desks from 8-5 but accomplishing little. I explained to Eugene that even thought I was not in the office for the full eight hours, each day that he was actually receiving more than 8 hours based on the results I was getting. He said he should have summarized that everything we covered in our previous meeting in writing to avoid future misunderstanding and he blamed himself for not following through. Eugene wanted it in writing I was not enrolling in summer school and if I chose to take a fall class I would have to make up the time a night. I told Eugene I felt like they brought me on in this new position when they knew things were tense and they were concerned over unenviable position Jackson had put them in. Eugene felt most comfortable micro-managing his people so he was compelled to call my time into question. I looked at Richard and asked him if he knew Eugene was unloading on me like this today. He responded no and then Richard said something positive. "Eugene, Nancy has done a great job."

The meeting adjourned with the understanding that we would all get together again with Stephanie Brown present. Stephanie would offer her interpretation of the April meeting and would monitor this meeting as the HR manager. As we all left the room I didn't make eye contact with Eugene. He called my name and tapped my shoulder and said we would work it out as if he knew he was making something out of nothing. I was unable to look at him because of the disrespectful, hostile environment he created and because he had questioned my character. As Richard and I walked back to our office he turned and commented, "I didn't see that coming at all." I dropped the class and achieving my degree was delayed. It was a terrible day.

A short time later our staff received this email from Eugene, the Vice Chancellor, sent this 4th of July happy message to his team:

From: Dunkas, Eugene
Sent: July 4, 2007
To: Staff
Subject: July 4th

I hope you and your families have a relaxing and safe July 4th holiday. Thank you for all that you do for this University!

Eugene Dunkas

I immediately left the campus after the meeting. I could no longer contain myself so I thought it best to disappear. Without delay I left Stephanie Brown a voice mail requesting a meeting on Thursday, the 5th. I requested for my husband, Doug, would be present to act as another set of ears to ensure correct comments and directions from our previous meeting with Eugene and how we move forward.

It is Just Too Much

Jerry was a best friend to us all with an extremely loving heart
her illness was a tragedy for our family and friends
but her death never tore us apart
I am feeling such a loss at this moment with little strength in my soul

my life is too overwhelming and I am losing
confidence in my personal goal
my confidence in leadership is starting to lose ground
I am feeling so exhausted and would love to just leave town

I approached Caroline Wilson my academic advisor to explain the topics discussed at Tuesday's meeting. She was floored by Eugene's outburst and was shocked the school issue had resurfaced. She encouraged me to call Stephanie as soon as possible and request a meeting to secure my position in II Summer 2008. I communicated I had already left her a voice mail and she offered for me to check my phone messages from her office line. I returned to work feeling somewhat insecure due to the alleged office gossip. Richard was out sick.

Stephanie returned my call promptly and made time for Doug and me to come in at 2:00. We thanked her for working us in, and I immediately shared with her the details of the Tuesday meeting in Eugene's office. She appeared shocked to learn of his outburst and stated she thought he had been dealing with several stressful situations. She continued to say she felt like I walked into a no-win situation with his mood being what it was. Stephanie curiously asked me why I was putting so much pressure on myself to finish within the year. Doug interrupted with this response:

"Where does Nancy work? A university. She comes to work every day in a high education environment and frankly, it was not until she was told by this University that her not having a degree was a problem. It was then she was told that people in her office were talking about her and it was there that malicious gossip was forcing her to go back to school and receive her degree."

- This university created this problem.
- This university promised its assistance for her to remain and work in Fort Worth.
- This university changed its commitment and agreement.
- My wife has gone above and beyond the requests while laws have been broken in the process. This is the result of the Jackson Hyde situation and I have had enough this nonsense.

I was so proud of my husband for defending my honor. I was disappointed I had to ask him to attend the meeting, but this had been an eighteen month battle and I didn't think I could bring this to an end without his assistance. I was the low man in the chain of command, and at the end of the day it was my word against my superiors. I reminded myself to document everything and continue to do my job.

But I was so tired and emotionally beaten down. At times I wanted to quit but this was not just about me; it was about my children and their education. I could feel my emotional stability slipping. Things had spiraled so out of control, but I knew deep down "Struggles Bring Blessings."

As requested, I called Richard at his home to report my progress for the week. I asked him if he had spoken to Eugene and he hadn't. He asked me if I had spoken to Stephanie and I told him yes. He reiterated that Eugene was firm on his decision about taking class during the day. I told him I would be willing to step aside and let Stephanie handle this situation.

I called Stephanie on her cell phone at 6:00 pm that evening to let her know what Richard had said. She suggested that we meet on Monday to discuss the next step of negotiations. I expressed the disappointment and betrayal I felt.

Hurt

My heart has been broken and I find it difficult to say
how people's low self mages can cause conflicts in so many ways
hard work and loyalty are the true virtues of the soul
but daily fighting the upstream current can take an emotional toll
when does one say I am done and move forward with a healthier mind
because dealing with unrealistic expectations with
superiors can just be so very unkind

Stephanie and I discussed the pertinent information for the upcoming meeting along with the best strategy for reaching a solution. She suggested that I remain silent during the entire meeting and allow her to speak on my behalf. The meeting was held in Eugene's conference room with Eugene, Stephanie, Richard and me present. The meeting opened with Eugene telling me he was not allowing me to take classes during the day offering multiple reasons supporting his decision. His comments were lengthy and detailed. Richard supported Eugene remarks by adding not only did he think I should not be allowed to take classes during the day, but he stated I shouldn't take classes in the evening because of the demands of my new position.

Stephanie and I sat in disbelief. As Richard finished his last statement, Stephanie started her rebuttal. She opened her argument with a riveting statement: "I think we should all agree that we are here because of the treatment Nancy received under you leadership. Because Nancy's job is not a regular 8-5 job because of appointments and events, she can attend classes during the day." Stephanie reminded everyone of the limited availability of the upper education classes and firmly added whether or not I attend classes in the evening was not anyone's business. How I use my time after 5:00 p.m. was my personal time and would and could not be monitored by the university. She was very professional and her remarks were aggressive and firm. With Stephanie's business-like statements and the direction of the meeting changed direction and the two men were silent.

I was in a state of pleasant shock as Stephanie defended me and our previous agreement relative to my education. It was at that exact moment that I finally felt substantiation of what I had been experiencing now over the last eighteen months. The confirmation I had and was still being bullied and a victim of the "boys" club mentality. Stephanie calmly stated: "Let's face it; we are all here because of the treatment Nancy received from Jackson Hyde." The room fell silent and the two men did not respond. Eugene looked directly at me and stated: "You have been very quiet, do you have anything to say?" I calmly said, "I find it interesting that everyone continues to tell me I can't raise a family, work, and go to school. My numbers are strong and I am on the honor roll. I have some where to go at 5 o'clock and frankly, I am getting tired of everyone trying to make me feel guilty for that."

Eugene looked at Stephanie and said, "I am hearing I should not be involved with this situation. So from this point forward Stephanie will monitor Nancy's progress. Nancy, you do what you need to do."

The meeting ended and I thanked Stephanie for her support and for making such a compelling argument on my behalf. "How will I ever thank you for what you just did for me?" I asked. She answered, "You just do for someone else what I have done for you today." Little did I know the responsibility that was given to me on that day!

Chapter 20
Debbie Downer

THE MENTAL STRESS OF THE confrontational at the meeting left me physically and emotionally exhausted for weeks. It also gave me a deep sadness in my heart. In addition to the pain I was angered that once again I was placed in another hostile situation. However; at the same time I was confident in my stand and satisfied that fairness had prevailed. I often wished I had completed my degree when I was supposed to but I also knew if I had finished on time I would have been like so many other women my age, college educated yet still not qualified to work in today's work force with all the technological advances. I knew in my heart there must be a reason for the many hurdles in my life and I continued to ponder where this demanding path was leading me. As stressful and sad as these times had been the last few years, they were still exciting because I was making progress with one of my life long goal – earning my degree.

My journey of education accentuated the emphasis I placed on a degree to my children. It was a legacy I wanted them to embrace and establish with the hope that the tradition of higher education and securing a college degree would continue and for generations to come. I decided if cancer was not going to kill me, I would dream and dream big. No one could ever make me feel inferior or intimidated about going back to school or achieving my other goals. Eugene Dunkas continued to maintain that I was not required to have my degree for my position even though many others did not share that opinion. I was no longer interested in his new strategy to create a new rule that my degree was no longer required for my position, thus creating fewer headaches for him with other employees wanting to do the same thing. I had to remind myself that his problems were not mine and I must stay focused on my responsibilities and obligations.

My sweet mother was in a constant state of sadness. With each conversation, her mood deteriorated further. I found myself with few words, which was a rare occurrence. One day, I picked up the phone and humorously referred to my mother as "Debbie Downer." She was a bit confused by the new nickname I had just given her. "Debbie" I stated, "until you can carry on a conversation without tears, then this will be your new name." For a brief moment, we both laughed and enjoyed some humor through our tears. My mother was the woman I had hoped to become, but in reality I think I am much more like my father. Mother had such a loving heart and her faith was felt by anyone who met her. Her love for the Lord and her family was the most important thing in her life. Every phone call was a tearful one, reminiscing about my older sister and her family.

The images of Terry began to resurface in each of our minds. We all slowly unlocked our guarded memories of her death through many lengthy phone calls. To this day, I am unable to recall the words I spoke at her memorial service, but I vividly remember the gospel singers as the familiar hymns often replay in my mind. The mental images of my parents' faces are entrenched forever in my mind. I will never forget the pain and despair I saw in their cloudy eyes that day.

I also remembered my brother Steve's incessant gasping for breath during the service. Doug and I initially thought Steve's erratic breathing was caused by emotion from the service, but soon realized that was not the case. Steve, a single man of forty-two years had never been married and his lifelong-dream was having a family and a large collie dog named "Mike." We all thought of Steve as a "mama's boy" and his love for our parents ran very deep.

With the week behind me I began coaching myself to stay on course with family and work in the days ahead. The Thanksgiving holidays came and went, and I was looking forward to another semester coming to a close and being able to cross off another six hours. The degree plan was starting to come together, but I reminded myself to "Take One Day at a Time" and break it down into "Baby Steps."

Our holiday debutante party for Bailey was approaching in four weeks and I was unsure how everything would come together. Our planning committee of four members was a competent group as we worked hard to stay in the budget and at the same time produce a wonderful event.

While one day, while eating lunch out I received a frantic call from the invitation addresser informing me that my party list had inaccurate data and the correct revisions must be made within the hour. I anxiously rushed back to my office to make the necessary changes. As I was approaching my office building I received another phone call from my brother in law informing me that my mother in law had suddenly collapsed in her home. He was frantic as he communicated her dire state. As a way of coping, my brain flipped the switch and I entered the "It's Business" mode. I immediately called in Samantha, my administrative assistant, and informed her of Mrs. Woodson's feared death. "I need your help," I helplessly stated. "I can feel my mother-in-law has just died, but I have to finish these addresses before I can call Doug." My mental state was in a complete lock down. Once again, our family was losing a family member and the sadness started to overwhelm me.

We shut the door, lifted the receiver off the hook, turned off my cell phone and entered a brief work mode. Within thirty minutes the corrections were complete. I knew it was time to reconnect myself with the "living" and face my husband's greatest fear and soon to be tragic reality.

Jo Ann Woodson was a woman of strength and had a pure love for her three boys. Her world consisted of her faith and her family and this was known to everyone who knew her. She was a pillar of strength and she too returned to school while in her forties for an additional college degree while caring for her homebound husband. They have now been married for forty-three years.

I thanked Samantha for her prompt and efficient assistance and I headed out the door to the hospital as Doug called me in route to the ER. He confirmed my worst fear. My mother in law had died instantly from a massive heart attack. Our family had suffered another loss just shy of the six-months after Terry's death.

Doug had lost his mother and his role model of forty-seven years. Bailey, Jay and Lawrence had loss their grandmother and I had loss a friend. I couldn't believe how I had grown to love this woman. It had become a pleasant surprise to experience our journey, from a forced family member into a real friendship. In the twenty-six years I knew this woman, we had lived through so many things including the marriages of Doug's younger brothers Patrick and Chad along with our three children totaling five grandchildren. Jo Ann was never given the opportunity to meet her sixth grandchild, Chad's son Ben. He entered this world five weeks after her death.

I had grown to love this woman over the years in our "inherited" relationship. Many times we shared different views and techniques in our mothering skills, but she had taught me how to love and care for my family. She knew the meaning and the importance of family and I will be eternally grateful for her wisdom, loving heart and her influence in my life.

I now had two guardian angels in heaven and I knew Terry had welcomed Jo Ann into God's everlasting kingdom. It comforted me to know they both had each other and we had them in our hearts. Dealing with processing the emotions of her death was another "hurdle" in our lives, but she was with her Maker and that was comforting to us.

I had two final exams to study and to prepare for within the upcoming weeks. I found it challenging to hold a focus as my mind would drift to Mrs. Woodson's last minutes on this earth. I would enter into deep thought, imagining the details of her last moments of her death. I often wondered if she knew she was dying and what her last thoughts might have been. Did she long to see her boys one more time and her husband of 43 years? Was she trying to fight her death in a negotiation with God? Or did she experience a calm peaceful departure? What was the focus of her last thoughts and did her journey on this earth live up to her expectations? My mind was full of curiosity regarding her departure from this world. What did her final moments reveal about her life? I could not get my mind passed her death, probably because her departure was unexpected.

At least with Terry's death, we all had a brief warning it was approaching and I was there when she left this world. I saw her death with my own eyes and it provided a healing process to see her departure from her physical and emotional pain. Terry was with her family in her dying moments, but Mrs. Woodson was all alone. She and her family didn't get the opportunity to say goodbye before she headed off to the place of perfection. It was painful and upsetting to visualize her last living moments falling to the floor in great pain and all alone.

Mother in Law

I have taken her life for granted
thinking her existence would never end
but when the day suddenly came
I felt so much loss to a loving kin
with her sudden death, I felt such an immediate pain
I loved her so dearly and how she kept our entire family sane
she held us all together and made each person feel right
she had the true gift of grace and love
as her legacy will fly high like a sailing kite
December 12, 2007

The loss of two close family members in less than six months seemed so unfair. Through it all I knew I had to keep my mind healthy and busy while remaining upbeat for my husband and our children. Pursuit of my degree, work and family kept me busy and my mind preoccupied which was a good thing for my mental and emotional state.

CHAPTER 21
Family Business

SUMMER '08 STARTED WITH A bang as I began the three-hour mini semester. Lawrence was studying for finals and excited about the start of her eight grade summer. Schoolwork had been a struggle for her throughout the years, but with support from both the principal and assistant principal we made it through. Doug and I were in regular contact with the school tracking her progress throughout Lawrence's seventh grade year. It was such a fun time to be a middle school student and she had been with this group of kids since kindergarten. Her dreams of being an eighth grade cheerleader for her school of nine years would become a reality in the fall.

We made a commitment to the school that Lawrence complete twenty hours of tutoring during the summer as a condition for her return to complete middle school. We were confident the additional work would benefit her future success.

The Memorial Day holiday marked the beginning of summer and our family members were headed in different directions. Bailey and Jay were starting their summer classes along with summer jobs. Bailey landed a sought after waitress job for a popular Mexican food restaurant and Jay was beginning his internship for a successful real estate developer. Lawrence was preparing for her academic tutoring sessions required by her school as well as organizing her friends to the pool. It was exciting to have two children employed and earning some extra spending money. Lawrence was spending her extra time at the barn with her horse, Chief, as well as assisting with barn responsibilities. I had decided to start a small photography business in my spare time and within a few short months it was starting to take off. My family was surprised that my picture taking hobby had turned into a business and was now earning money. Things were looking up for the Woodson family; perhaps our new guardian angels were doing their thing in love and support of us.

Lawrence began her new tutoring obligations with a positive attitude and a spring in her step. We received a letter from the assistant principle confirming her promotion to eighth grade with the completion of the twenty hours of summer work.

June 5, 2008

Mr. and Mrs. Doug Woodson
5418 Collingwood Cove
Somewhere, Texas 22222

Dear Mr. and Mrs. Woodson,

I am writing as a follow-up to our conversations regarding Lawrence's need for academic support this summer. As we discussed throughout the year, Lawrence's status on Academic Warning requires that she complete summer work...

Per the school's handbook, students are only allowed to use summer remediation once and still return to Private School without petitioning the Head of School. Below are the guidelines Lawrence must meet to satisfy the school's requirements for summer support...

Sincerely,
Cindy Heard
Academic Support Services
Assistant Middle School Division Head

David Jacobs
Head of Middle School

CC: Dickson Short

Doug and I emphasized to Lawrence the importance of her ownership in this additional learning opportunity and that it would be her responsibility to get to each session in the neighborhood on time by foot or by bike. Our children taking sole responsibility for their academic work has been a priority for us. Although; their grades would have been stronger with our assistance, we believed it was not in their long term best interest to assist them to the extent that many parents did. Several years ago I came to the realization this strategy can be extremely effective as Doug reminded me not to reward the children for things they should do for themselves because it reduces the value of the accomplishment thus robbing them of their self esteem. The outcome of this philosophy hopefully results in a lasting learning experience. Middle school was a time to let our children experience a failing grade for an effortless effort. For in reality middle school grades did not appear on their transcript, so a lesson learned was much more important ......or so we thought.

The days were growing longer and the Texas heat was intensifying in its traditional manner. It was strange for us not attending sporting events as Jay was now in college.

The house was quite busy with children coming and going and the two dogs wearing out their welcome as usual. One Sunday afternoon I found myself not concentrating while steering down the driveway. Instead I was focusing on not hitting the "beast" (this is how I fondly refer to our beagle, Copper). I suddenly heard a loud noise. The bushes began to shake as my driver side mirror slammed into the electronic gate. I hit on my breaks and jumped out of my car to inspect the damage, first to my vehicle and then to the gate. To my surprise, my car was dent free, but the new wrought iron gate was stuck in the open position. I waited a few hours to tell Doug of the mishap, hoping to have repaired it on my own. I knew me fixing the gate would be a long shot, but I wanted to avoid his wrath over another expensive repair and at the very least I hoped that he would appreciate my effort.

I entered the bedroom and timidly shared the story of the broken gate. Doug was not amused at my attempt to dramatize the event in fact; it's safe to say he was pissed. The afternoon was moving towards an F4 without any of the children at home. Doug's mood was going south by the minute. I decided it was best to cancel our evening dinner plans with another couple. It was best for the both of us for me to leave him alone with his mail and the remote control.

Sunday evening brought little conversation between us so I chose to call my mother for our regular chat. We had been talking for about an hour about every topic we could think of. She reminisced about my childhood days that included tearful stories of Terry. It was too much for one woman to bear; her cross was becoming heavier with each day. The conversations would start off positive but always develop into a grave discussion referring to mother as "Debbie Downer" to lighten the mood. We often broke into laughter from our tears. It was a tender time.

As I was wrapping up the conversation with "Debbie", Doug suddenly came around the corner asking me to get off the phone. I motioned to him to wait a minute, but he insistently demanded my attention. "We have a real problem!" he said and I had no idea what he was talking about. With a look of concern on his face, he handed me a letter from the Headmaster of Lawrence's school. He straightforwardly stated, "Lawrence has been dismissed from school." Not sure what in the world he was talking about, I reached for the letter and it read it promptly.

Dickson Short, the Headmaster had kicked her out of school with a letter just sixty days prior to the start of her last year in middle school. The letter was dated Thursday, June 19, 2008. It arrived in our mailbox on Saturday, June 21st and was discovered by Doug as he casually opened the mail on Sunday, June 22nd. This letter came as a complete shock to us and didn't make sense. Two weeks earlier we had received a letter from the assistant principal stating that Lawrence had satisfied her requirements and was to report to school in August as a member of the eight grade class.

The second time I read the letter aloud and was speechless, a rare occurrence for me. As I was slowly recited each word to mother who was attentively listening to the harsh decision on the other end of the phone when all of a sudden she burst into tears and cried out for Lawrence. Mother was so upset because she knew her emotional state would be greatly affected by being dismissed from the school she had attended for eight years; the only school she knew.

I glanced into Doug's eyes and saw a look of concern and sadness I had rarely seen. He was a heart broken man with the look of a damaged soul. He was devastated. I couldn't even respond to the madness. It was as if I was having an out of body experience. Once again, I did not know what to do with an adverse challenge that had presented itself out of nowhere. Initially, I found myself trying to be emotionally supportive for my husband I racked my brain for a potential solution as I knew I couldn't get upset because he was not in a good place. It was surprising to have our roles reversed, but I was feeling the strength to help carry his disappointment. Typically that was his job and role. The fact that we did not receive any warning about this life changing decision was disrespectful and uncaring to our child and our family. After many years of family history with this educational institution we are not even worthy of a phone call regarding this abrupt and poorly timed decision? Subsequently, within a few weeks, our question was answered: the reason we didn't get a phone call or meeting was because this was the decision and action of one man, Dickson Short.

We had been following the direction of the Middle School Principal, David Jacobs, who had taken a special interest and seemed determined to get Lawrence through eighth grade. He told us in January Lawrence was able to do the work and could successfully complete the Middle School program. In my opinion, middle school is the time when a child should take ownership and responsibility in their grades and learn to become an independent student. We never did any of their work or special projects however, we were available to assist but that was it. We all agreed it would be best for her academically, emotionally and socially. After all, Doug was a graduate of this private school, along with his younger brother, cousin and our other two children. Our loyalty to this school was steadfast and apparently not to be reciprocated? How could one man have this power to release a child without discussion well beyond the deadline for admission at other private schools? The most compelling question to me: Where was the compassion for my child and our family after losing two family members in the last twelve months? Lawrence had lost her grandmother and aunt in the last year and that stress alone has a devastating effect on a child.

There were so many questions running through our minds and on a Sunday night, we knew it would be another twelve hours before we would have any answers. I suggested we both take a little something to help us sleep and tackle this "hurdle" full force the next day with rested minds. Doug was in agreement and we focused on making the remainder of the night a peaceful one.

The following morning there was little conversation and a feel of tension was in the air. We both rushed to our respective offices to get our work duties under control so we could focus on getting our daughter reinstated in her school. We were determined to face this issue head on in an effort to learn the specific reasons for this pronouncement. It was a mutual decision that we not yet share the disturbing news with Lawrence because she was about to leave for a long weekend trip to New York and Nantucket with one of her closest friends.

Doug sent an email to the Headmaster, requesting a face to face meeting. He tried to use a light humor in reference to my breaking the driveway gate.

From: Doug Woodson
Sent: Monday, > 6/23/2008
To: Short, Dickson
Cc: Jacobs, David; Heard, Cindy; Woodson, Nancy
Subject: RE: Lawrence

Yesterday I was surprised and shocked after reading your letter of June 19, 2008, which we received on Saturday June 21. It capped off what had proved to be a pretty "shitty" day. Heather (your administrative assistant) I apologize.

May we meet on this at your earliest convenience? Any time, any day, Anywhere; please let me know. With all the efforts that have been put forward we have seen marked progress from Lawrence; progress that did not get reflected in her last round of grades. Not allowing Lawrence to at least finish her middle school experience with the only class of children she has ever known, will be devastating. Not to mention the fact that it is too late to get her into any private school due to the timing of this.

I have so much to say and prefer to say it in person; if given the opportunity. Thank you.

Dickson returned this disturbing response:

From: Short, Dickson
Sent: Monday, June 23, 2008
To: Doug Woodson
Cc: Jacobs, David
Subject: Re: Lawrence

D
I'm sorry the situation caused you to have a shitty day!
You received the information in as timely a fashion as possible. I don't
think doors are closed at other schools at this time since my assistant
told me she can make calls for you if you like.

My letter of April 14 was very clear on the school's position. Rather than
meeting with me to debate a point I will not debate, timing says your
efforts should be on working with my assistant to find the right match.

If you need to call a school I am more than willing to help in that
regard.
D

Doug and I were on the phone when Dickson's email arrived in his
inbox. He calmly said, "Here's his response." Doug opened his message
and started to read the disappointing words. With each word he read,
his volume declined into a more somber tone. He recited one sentence
a few times: "Rather than meeting with me to debate a point I will not
debate........."

"Oh my goodness," I replied. "He is a bully! Doug, can't you hear that
in his words? He is bullying you. The number one sign of a bully is they
will not negotiate with you and their word is law without discussion." I
could not believe this was happening. Once again, a bully was pushing
me and my family around.

Doug's hesitated for a moment then said, "You know. I think you
are correct," I need to gather my thoughts and call you back in a bit."
His voice was cracking as Doug realized exactly what he was up against.
It was a disappointing moment for him to realize he had no power or
control and the school he felt such an allegiance to felt little, or perhaps,
no allegiance to him. The conversation ended and I knew my husband
had entered a dark place full of sadness and he needed some time to sort
this out.

CHAPTER 22
This is Crap

T HE MINUTES TICKED AWAY AS I waited for Doug to call me back. I knew he was just sitting in his office feeling dejected over the chain of events. I knew he was missing his mother terribly and it broke my heart that he couldn't pick up the phone and call her about Lawrence's dismissal. He rarely spoke of her sudden departure from our family, but he certainly valued her opinion on several matters and he would have benefitted from her counsel on this school issue. The in-laws had spent many years on that campus with two sons having graduated from the school and they having attended multiple "Grandparent Days" with their four grandchildren.

When Doug returned my phone call he confidently stated the importance of a face to face meeting with Headmaster Short. He pulled up all prior correspondence from the school as well as every report card and progress report within the last twenty-four months that he meticulously kept in a file in his office.

According to a letter from Dickson two months prior, requiring that Lawrence maintain a 70 average or above in the five core classes. Doug accessed Lawrence's grades from the school website and calculated her yearly average. The resulting average of all classes was 74. He then figured her five core classes which averaged 70.3. According to Dickson's calculation, she received a 68.4.

Unbeknown to us the school had not yet posted to the student's final grades that include final exam scores. Keep in mind school had been out for two weeks at this point so we assumed the website was current and up-to-date.

Naturally Doug was encouraged by his calculation and based on that insisted he be given the opportunity to appeal the dismissal decision. He sent this request for a personal meeting:

From: Doug Woodson
Sent: Monday, June 23, 2008
To: Dickson Short
Cc: Jacobs, David; Heard, Cindy; Woodson, Nancy
Subject: RE: Lawrence

A debate is not what I had in mind. I would like to meet with you on this, and I feel that I deserve that opportunity. At your convenience, please let me know.

While waiting for Dickson's response Doug decided to contact a person who believed in Lawrence's ability and expended a lot of time and effort throughout this entire process, David Jacobs, Middle School Principal. Throughout the school year, on his suggestion, Lawrence, Doug and me had meet with Mr. Jacobs three times to monitor her progress and discuss what we could do to get her successfully through seventh grade. Mr. Jacobs was a patient, well intentional man who seemed to take a special interest in Lawrence. He was invested in Lawrence's success and that came out in our meeting.

Doug sent this email requesting for his assistance:

From: Doug Woodson
Sent: Monday, June 23, 2008
To: Jacobs, David
Cc: Woodson, Nancy
Subject: Lawrence

...I am aware that only Dickson can reverse the decision that has been made, and I understand the decision and the criteria that preceded it.

Lawrence's situation brought back my feelings of my academic struggles. The truth was I was feeling responsible for her not making the grade. I found it so ironic that I had gone back to school expecting to set an example for my children on the importance of their education, and now my child had been kicked out of school. Not only was Lawrence not in school, but we as a family felt abandoned by the school that had promoted her success for eight years.

Failure

*I am scared I have failed my child with my selfish agenda ways
working and going back to school
demanded too much time away from Lawrence with an
unexpected consequence we are experiencing today
I thought was setting a strong example
but its lasting effects interfered with my parental time
as I truly hoped a strong work ethic would encourage
my children to develop their own confident mind
I am feeling guilty as a mother with her dismissal from her school
maybe I should have done her work for her and checked the
websites for scheduled assignments like other mother's do
I would have at least had my child in a school
with her friends from the early years
I am feeling such a loss
but at thirteen years old, she should be a happy
teenager with all her childhood peers*

The late date of dismissal left us with inadequate time to plan and find the right fit for Lawrence academically, socially, and emotionally. Headmaster Short's token offer of having his assistant make some phone calls to other schools was designed to save face and meant nothing to us. An experienced private school administrator expected us to be grateful and ask him for assistance after kicking our daughter out of school under questionable circumstances two weeks after the school year had ended? Certainly not.

Oftentimes I felt guilty for going back to work and school due to the time it took me away from doing things for my family. Lawrence's dismissal brought back bad memories of my academic challenges which fueled my guilt. Was the cost worth the reward? Going back to work despite all the issues was the best thing I could have done for myself. Earning my degree in conjunction with my work reinvigorated me and made me a better person. But just like all women who achieve success outside the household, I succumbed to guilt from time to time. And when I had these attacks of guilt I remind myself to break it down into "Baby Steps" and "Take One Day at a Time."

Doug and I raised three independent children to have a strong sense of right and wrong with an understanding that actions have consequences. Once again I knew this struggle would bring a blessing and this was another "hurdle" in our life, but at the time I was unsure of the emotional and physical outcome. I reminded Doug the goals and objectives we set ourselves in order to be successful parents and I stated it in this email to Doug:

From: Woodson, Nancy
Sent: Wednesday, June 25, 2008
To: Doug Woodson
Subject: Lawrence

I think we have to remind ourselves that we are raising independent children. We don't do their homework, check the website for their assignments, pack their camp trunks and we make them earn most of their spending money. Maybe we aren't the "private school" typical parents.....and really that is not a bad thing. We have always told our children.....do your best and that is all we ask for. We are in private school for the full experience. For him to turn away a 13-year-old girl eight weeks before school starts...with just a letter/no call is unspeakable. Remember what JC Watts said... Dickson was not part of the equation when we started at this campus and his vision may not be ours.....just a thought!

From: Doug Woodson
Sent: Wednesday, June 25, 2008
To: Woodson, Nancy
Subject: RE: Lawrence

Now that is very well spoken; maybe you can be an author. I agree with everything you have said.
Philippians 4:11-12 drives me.

A professor at the local university was kind enough to speak with me and offer his advice as an expert in the College of Education. He expressed his concern with the timing of our child's release from our family school as explained it was a delicate time for a middle school emotional, physically and socially. He was aware of Headmaster Short's reputation but didn't know him on a personal level. He questioned his motive of releasing her during her last year of middle school and simply offered his opinion as a man exerting too much power and ego. The wounds from Jackson Hyde with my employment experience in the past two years had resurfaced in my mind. I felt as if God was offering me a gift to have Doug experience Dickson's bullying. For the first time he was understanding the hell I had been experiencing by the abuse of power from Jackson Hyde a short time earlier and it made me feel as if we had both walked through that fire together.

Dickson responded to Doug's request for a meeting seventy-two hours later on Thursday, June 26th, less than sixty days before the start of the next school year. Doug also received a phone call from the middle school principal, David Jacobs, while he was out of town but out of his office when he called back. Doug sent an email to the assistant principal, Cindy Heard bringing to light the inconsistencies between her letter and Dickson's.

From: Doug Woodson
Sent: Wednesday, June 25, 2008
To: Heard, Cindy
Cc: Jacobs, David
Subject: Lawrence

I re-read the recent letters: yours dated June 2008 and Dickson's dated June 19, 2008. Clearly it was your understanding as you drafted this letter (and my understanding as I read it) that Lawrence would be attending your school in the fall. Not to mention the fact that the re-enrollment contract was signed and my check was cashed...
Lawrence's grades in the 5 core courses for the entire year average out to 70.3...

Doug J. Woodson

Not surprisingly, Cindy never responded. She knew all the history, the recent chain of events and the type of man she worked for.

In the meantime Doug reached out to a couple close friends about the approach he should take in this very unusual situation. Doug's emotions were running high and the many long hours he was putting into preparing for our daughter's defense was taking its toll on him. I reminded him of my experience with working with a bully. It is a marathon, not a sprint! One will rarely or never experience success immediately. It is a long, exhausting process, one of mental focus and detailed documentation.

I was trying to look for the blessing to this unexpected "hurdle" in our lives when I suddenly felt a ray of light. For the longest time, when I was working in a hostile environment, experiencing my boss's mood swings, irrational demands, verbal and email abuse, Doug would tell me to just ignore him and do my job. At that time he didn't fully understand what I was going through, but through this experience with Dickson he grasped the extent of my past struggle. Basically the same thing that happened to Doug previously happened to me. He was finally feeling the pain, heart break and frustration I had felt in the last two years. Was it coincidence that we encountered very similar treatment from two very different men that shared a dysfunctional approach to getting their way? I didn't realize it at the time, but as I reflect back, I am reminded that God's timing is perfect and I should not question His direction and simply follow His path. These experiences made our family come together and grow as a family unit. My journey had become my family's journey and we were all heading down that yellow brick road together for the same purpose.....loving and supporting each other.

Maybe I really am Dorothy heading down that yellow brick road. I am not really sure how my life has gotten to this point. How did a stay-at-home mom with three children who hadn't finished college with limited work experience become an employee and a student at a major university? I think I surprised myself to a certain extent. It is truly amazing what we can accomplish if we just put our minds to it and are willing to make sacrifices to reach our goals. Just as my husband always says, "Keep your eye on the ball."

Doug reached out to one of Lawrence's strongest advocates, David Jacobs. He had always encouraged us regarding Lawrence's academic development with a positive attitude yet realistic approach. As the school year progressed David expressed confidence in her increased capabilities and was confident that we embrace her ability and effort to conquer the curriculum. He accurately identified the areas that needed special attention and offered effective strategies to attack them. Doug hoped to get his insight and opinion to prepare for the meeting.

From: "Doug Woodson"
To: Jacobs, David
Cc: Nancy Woodson
Sent: June 26, 2008
Subject: Lawrence

As I prepare for my meeting with Dickson in the morning: reading all the letters, emails, report cards, progress reports, etc., my thoughts turn to you and the firm, yet caring guidance you have afforded us. I feel strongly that Lawrence has earned and deserves the right to return to school for her 8th grade year. Based on our meetings I am confident that you share this opinion…

…Finishing middle school with the only group of kids (and the only school) she has ever known is certainly the best for Lawrence. The comment is often made that we must do what is best for the child. Even though the curriculum of our school may be too challenging for Lawrence there is no one who could convince me that placing her in an unfamiliar environment with children she does not know for her 8th grade year is what is best for her. What is best for her is to be afforded the opportunity to finish middle school at her school…

Doug J. Woodson

Doug was running out of time to hear from David for his insight on what to expect from Dickson. Doug and I were confident David would contact Dickson and communicate to him what he had been sharing with us throughout the year. David was invested in Lawrence's progress and development and we anticipated he would motivate Dickson to reconsider.

As word spread of Lawrence's dismissal several people called Doug to find out if what they had heard was true and some shared similar stories of Dickson's bullying tactics in exerting his power. Once these reports of multiple bullying events were confirmed by our conversations with the victims, I knew it would be very difficult to gain support.

According to Dickson, it was a unanimous decision between three faculty members including himself, Cindy Heard and David Jacobs. Doug and I found the statement from Dickson not to be true as evidenced by his letter to us dated June 5, 2008. Dickson told Doug that Lawrence had shared with him several things that she had not shared with us. He said Lawrence told him she was stressed out and feared failing academically. Doug immediately knew this wasn't the case, as Lawrence rarely exhibited any anxiety regarding her schoolwork and never showed signs of stress or fear. In fact, Dickson's statement couldn't have been farther from the truth. Lawrence was the first out of bed in our house every school day, often dressed and in the kitchen making breakfast as Doug and I were getting our first cup of coffee. Despite her academic struggles she always looked forward to school because she is a "people" person; she loved her friends and is very social. This statement was a failed attempted by Dickson to build his case with us that Lawrence should leave; he saw the opportunity to rid this class of a student that would drag the overall grade point down and he jumped on it. What a reaction and pain he was bringing on to her? Life had thrown another hurdle in our path and the challenge now was to clear the wooden obstacle and somehow turn this injustice into an opportunity. However, we still had two questions to ask: when and how would we tell Lawrence about the blind side dismissal? It was difficult to imagine her initial reaction about being dismissed from the school she had grown to love and a faculty she had come to trust and respect through their guidance. Frankly, I was not finding much strength to fight.

> *I could feel the exhaustion in my heavy breathing, as I started to see the small white line in the distance. The group was running at a full speed, as I felt my feet becoming heavier and heavier with each step. My pace was starting to weaken as my legs were starting to take a slow runner's stride. I had little desire to continue on. Suddenly, I felt a burst of energy overtake my body. I was becoming energized with my personal pursuit and I could see the end in sight. I could see the finish line in my full vision and I felt empowered to complete the task at hand. I suddenly realized I was not competing with the other runners, but with myself. I was running towards a goal and through the obstacles and fear of failing, I persevered and stayed focused on the task. I could feel that I was going to finish and for the first time during this race, I could envision my success!*

Doug and I were anxious to hear from David because we knew he would continue to be Lawrence's strongest supporter. We felt confident he would remind Dickson of Lawrence's progress, excellent attitude and would defend his prior statements of her ability to complete 8th grade successfully. To our surprise David's position and opinions had suddenly changed.

(sic)
From: Jacobs, David
Sent: Thursday, June 26, 2008
To: Doug Woodson
Subject: Re: Lawrence

Dear Doug and Nancy,

I feel terrible that I am not able to be there during this time. I hope the two of you know what a huge Lawrence fan I am. What I want for Lawrence is for her to be in a program, which can better support the areas she struggles in and emphasizes the areas that we all appreciate about her. Though it Hurts me to say, I do not think this place for her. The 8th grade curriculum is much more strenuous than this year's. I do not think that would be an environment where she would feel good about herself. I know this would cause some short- term duress, but I think it would be the best in the long run. I know this is not what you wanted to hear. As I write this, I fear that it may cost me the respect of a student whom I admire and a family I respect, but it is as honest as I can be.

Regretfully,
David

At that moment, Doug and I knew Dickson had made it clear to David that Lawrence was out and we had lost all previous support to get her reinstated. The bully had succeeded in the short term. He had flexed his muscles to rid himself of an average student and demanded his employees stand by his edict without question of further decision. All promises verbally and in legal documentation would not be honored or respected by the school. Dickson's reign of command made this clear. The hard work and consistent efforts of his subordinated in support of Lawrence meant nothing to him not to mention what we had been told verbally and promised in writing.

From: Doug Woodson

Sent: Thursday, June 26, 2008
To: 'Jacobs, David'
Cc: 'Woodson, Nancy'
Subject: RE: Lawrence

...We believe firmly that Lawrence deserves the right to return and if you do not share that opinion, that is OK. Rest assured I will do everything in my power to see to it that she finishes middle school where she is. Lawrence finished the year with an average of 70.3. Dickson's letters stated that this is the criteria for return and I expect him to stand by that. I hope to have this worked out in the morning.

Doug Woodson

Dickson had given up on Lawrence and placed our family in an untenable situation. The way he handled this was unspeakable. We receive a letter two weeks after school had ended after being told verbally and in writing that she was a part of the 8th grade class and we don't get so much as a phone call? Doug documented everything including his meeting with Dickson together with all the letters, emails and notes of conversations. My husband has an attention to detail that annoys the hell out of me, but in some situations has merit. This was one of those situations.

The true sign of a bully is that they will not listen to varying opinions nor negotiate or open the issue for discussion. I was having a Déjà vu moment here. Dickson had a reputation as a tyrant with his subordinates that clearly revealed his abusive management style that had been going on for years. His subordinates openly referred to his emails as "howlers" which was unknown to me, but through this experience I was informed of this by several of his faculty members.

I had some insight into this type of behavior courtesy of the Jackson Hyde situation. God's plan was revealed to me by the similarities of my situation with Jackson and Doug's experience with Dickson. The way each of them handled very different challenges and circumstance was eerily similar, and I felt somewhat validated witnessing my husband standing up for Lawrence and my family.

Doug sent Dickson a detailed synopsis of their meeting and then forwarded the email to one of his best friends.

From: Doug Woodson
Sent: Saturday, June 28, 2008

To: Short, Dickson
CC: Woodson, Nancy; Boone, Pam
Subject: June 26th meeting

I appreciate you taking the time to meet with me last Thursday at your office regarding your decision to deny Lawrence's re-enrollment for 8th grade. To summarize our conversation and confirm my understanding, we discussed the following:

1) GPA: I brought it to your attention that her annual academic average was 70.25...
2) June 2008 letter: I brought up the letter drafted by the Assistant Middle School Head which I received on June 5. As you know, the letter outlined the school's policy for re-enrollment for children on academic warning and the requirement that she have at least 20 hours of academic support this summer...
3) Contract and payment: I asked you about the presence of our signed re-enrollment contract and the cashing of my check, and you said "you can't play that card"...
4) Your meetings with Lawrence: You brought up that you and she met on 3 or 4 occasions during the school year and that in those meetings she expressed things to you that she had never expressed to us. You said that she is "tired of the struggle" and that she "tells us the things that we want to hear." I then told you that she is a very happy kid with strong self esteem...

...Members of your staff agree that she can make it through 8th grade; they all have told me so. I know it is hard to reverse a decision already made, but in this situation it is better for Lawrence, her family and you, that you do. You can reverse this decision immediately and very few people will ever know about it, which is certainly in everyone's best interest.

Doug's friend suggested that this email be forwarded to members of the Executive Committee and he consented. We knew our chance for success was a long shot, but knew the facts were on our side and perhaps an appeal would work.

From: Doug Woodson
Sent: Sunday, July 06, 2008
To: Boone, Pam; School Board Executive Committee Members
Cc: Woodson, Nancy
Subject: Lawrence

Just today we told Lawrence about the recent events. After she stopped crying (30 minutes plus) she came downstairs and said that she didn't understand why. Before I gave an answer I asked her what she didn't understand and she said that she made 70 and that is what Mr. Short said she had to do to return. I asked her how she knew she had finished with 70 and she said she added up her grades. I then asked her how she knew how to do that and she said that in their 2nd meeting she asked Mr. Short how to do it and that he showed her how to calculate her grade average. This is important because he has told me and you that my calculation is not accurate and that this is: "Not open for debate" is the reference he made to the grade point average...

...My position is that she be reinstated. You both know me well enough to know that I do not like to make waves, but at the same time I stand up for what is right. The longer this goes on, the more my resolve strengthens. It is not my intention to impose upon you or place you in a difficult situation. Thank you for your time and consideration. I am available to discuss this further tonight or tomorrow.

Doug's well written email scripted out the high points and low points of the meeting referenced correspondence from the school with a logical request for reconsideration. In addition to forwarding the email to Dickson, Doug sent a documentation of the events to the Board of Trustees:

From: Doug Woodson
Sent: Tuesday, July 08, 2008
To: Boone, Pam
Cc: Woodson, Nancy
Subject: Lawrence

Nancy, Lawrence and I sincerely appreciate your time and efforts in considering this unfortunate situation...

I would like to talk to you; however, I do not want you to feel uncomfortable so that is why I am reaching out via email.

Pam Boone was the active Chairman of the Board of our school and an avid supporter of Dickson Short. We had a child in the same graduating class but our paths would seldom cross. I felt Pam being a mother would encourage Dickson to protect Lawrence as a thirteen year-old girl, as well as a student who had suffered two tremendous losses.

From: Boone, Pam
Sent: Tuesday, July 08, 2008
To: Doug Woodson
Subject: RE: Lawrence

Doug,
Thanks for your message. I would be happy to set up a time to talk with you; would Thursday be convenient? ...
Pam

Once again, I set myself up with high expectations that Pam would step up for Lawrence only to find myself disappointed. She was not only coming to the rescue but toted the company line.

From: Doug Woodson
Sent: Tuesday, July 08, 2008
To: Woodson, Nancy
Subject: FW: Lawrence

This response reminds me of Dickson's; can't talk now; let's talk in 48 hours ...

I decided to take a week of vacation time to tour schools and spend time with Lawrence because she was not in a good place. I had left several messages with the school office for Lawrence's transcripts and three days later I received a phone call from David Jacobs. He informed me of his efforts to gather the requested information which was necessary for admission to any other school. I asked if he would allow me a few opinions on what had transpired while I had him on the phone and he graciously accepted. I told him how I thought he had "sold out my daughter" and our family to save his job. My emotions escalated with each word because I knew he believed in Lawrence. I also knew he had been put in a position by his boss to abandon everything Lawrence had accomplished and was working towards.

From: Doug Woodson
Sent: Saturday, July 12, 2008
To: Jacobs, David

Subject: RE: Transcript

Thank you, David, but from my view you were not saddened enough to stick up for Lawrence when your boss wanted her gone and that is extremely disappointing. The way this was handled by Dickson and the emotional distress it has caused is beyond belief. We will move on, and as with all devastating situations the passage of time will heal our Hurt and distress and the pain will slowly go away. Dickson (and now you) will always be remembered by how this was handled, and that will never go away...

So many emotions we were all experiencing with the disrespectful treatment headed by one man. The true disappointment throughout this entire experience was Dickson's bullying management of his faculty that was being viewed by our family. Not to mention how within a few days Lawrence had lost all previous support to continue her education by this institution and her confidence level was in jeopardy. However going against a bully and his rule can have devastating consequences to staff members and their future employment. David was our strongest advocate for Lawrence but his weakness to his bully boss was the final blow to her academic success at this private school. We found ourselves in an impossible situation.

From: Doug Woodson
Sent: Saturday, 7/30/2008
To: Short, Dickson
CC: Woodson, Nancy; Boone, Pam
Subject: June 26th meeting

You have no idea how much distress and pain you have inflicted on me and my family. As of this date, Lawrence has not been admitted to a private school...

The following day Lawrence and I were sitting in my office as I logged on to the school website. A message stated my password was inactive. The communication was not in error; my access had been deliberately discontinued. Lawrence gave me her information to log on to only to find out she too had been locked out of the system as well. I was on the phone with Doug while this was taking place and he didn't believe me so he offered his alumni access password. I waited on the line as he emailed me his information only to discover his password would not allow access to the site either. Doug immediately sent an email to the administration asking for assistance and was directed to the person that manages the website.

From: Woodson, Doug
Sent: Friday, August 01, 2008
To: Tanner, Sue
Cc: Short, Dickson; Woodson, Nancy; Woodson, Bailey; Woodson, Jay

My user name and password are not noted below; would you please send again.
Doug J. Woodson

Doug received this response to his request for assistance.

From: Tanner, Sue
Sent: Saturday, August 01, 2008
To: Woodson, Doug
Cc: Short, Dickson; Woodson, Nancy; Woodson, Bailey; Woodson, Jay

Doug,
Please contact Dickson Short in regards to your inquiry.

Thank you,
Sue Tanner
Administrative Assistant

Dickson had locked out our entire family from the school's website. I knew my parent status would be revoked and Lawrence would lose her web site access as a student, but Doug, Bailey and Jay were graduates of the school so blocking their access did not make sense. To make matters worse I soon discovered that Doug, Bailey and Jay had been removed from the alumni registry on the website as if they had never been a part of the school. A good friend of mine brought this to my attention and I verified it by accessing the website with her password. I immediately called Doug, gave him her password and he accessed the website and printed the pages that provided evidence of what had been done at the direction of Dickson.

From:	Doug Woodson
Sent:	Saturday, August 02, 2008
To:	Short, Dickson
Cc:	Boone, Pam; Woodson, Nancy; Woodson, Bailey; Woodson, Jay

Attachments: ▢ Password Request

This morning I was informed by a friend who is an ex-Board member that my two children and I have been removed from the Alumni Roster on the school's website. I was not able to confirm this event this morning because you previously instructed Heather your administrative assistant to deny me access to the school website. I talked to Pam Boone about this just an hour ago and she told me that I need to take this up with you and the Alumni office. I have since gained access to the site and have in fact confirmed that my name (class of 1979), Bailey Woodson (class of 2005) and Jay Woodson (class of 2007) have been removed from the site.

Please let me know why you have done this and if you plan for this to be permanent. Thanks

Apparently his bullying tactics were not enough; he was compelled by vindictiveness because his authority and decisions had been called into question. He was sending Doug a message and his word was law and there was no room for anything else.

Where did the loyalty go? How could the trustees of the school allow this type of treatment to one of its own? Granted the Headmaster of any private school must have total control to hire and fire and dismiss any student, but what happens when the person in charge with all this authority abuses his power? Not a word. No one person or any single situation can disrupt the authority and administration of this private school. This was the mentality we were fighting, and the Board of Trustees backed Dickson despite the compelling facts of what transpired. We knew the trustees had acknowledged the seriousness of the situation when we found out a special meeting had been called. It was summertime and school was out so few were focused on the matters of school.

According to a trustee present at the special meeting conference call, Dickson asked the question if the Board would reverse his decision. Legally, the trustees cannot reverse the decision due to the Headmaster's contract and the school by-laws. The trustees knew it was incumbent on them to act responsibly in support of the school and its community. This put them in a tough position.

One who has authority over another and allows an abuse of power is just as guilty as the perpetrator. JC Watts said it best at a local business event in the spring of 2008:"When too much ego and power come together, it is a devastating combination." Leadership is a privilege. It should be held in the highest regard, by its leader with accountability, as the leading principle. It is the responsibility of each internal society to set guidelines with stated by-laws with equal opportunity to all individuals. Leadership should always be delivered with respect, grace and dignity. We should hold our leaders to this standard regardless of race, color, religion, sex or national origin.

What I will always wonder is did Headmaster Dickson remove my family from the website before or after sending this email?

From: Short, Dickson
Sent: Thursday, July 31, 2008
To: Doug Woodson
Cc: Boone, Pam
Subject: Re:

D

...I know how much you and your family would love Lawrence to return to this school. It is difficult to tell families that this is not the right place for everyone. Lawrence has struggled here for many years! You must recognize that fact as I know you do. During her time here she used every available academic support system the school offers. She was on academic warning or probation six of eight marking periods and she asked for more in her appeal to me. However, she did not end the year the way you or I had hoped she would. As the academic leader of this institution it is my responsibility to see that the school follows procedures outlined in our public information about academic preparedness. It is also my responsibility to hold true to the fact that this school was established as an academic institution of the highest regard. With that charge and responsibility it is left to me to uphold and maintain those academic standards.

Finally, please know that this is not about my pride. It is about following agreements made with families and about following the rules set forth in school guidelines, handbooks, contracts, and academic curricula. It is about making sure that we treat everyone honestly, and fairly even when the outcomes are not the ones we would have desired.

Doug, Lawrence is a wonderful young lady. When I met with her in April I was impressed with her and how she handled herself. She will do great things in her life that will make you as proud as a parent can be. I wish her only the very best and stand ready any way I can to help her move forward. If I could offer on bit of advice parent to parent, help Lawrence move forward! Causing your anger with me and the school to be a public issue is not helping the one person we are all here to help.

Doug replied to Dickson's email:

From: Doug Woodson
Sent: Fri 8/1/2008
To: Short, Dickson
Cc: Boone, Pam; Woodson, Nancy
Subject: Lawrence

...Regarding your comments about being the "academic leader" of an "academic institution of the highest regard" absolutely you are and absolutely it is. I have read all the school documents that you cite below plus the By-Laws of the school, and I do not question your authority. I do question the manner within which you exercise that authority and your blatant disregard for promises made and diligent efforts expended to achieve a goal shared by Lawrence, her mother and I, and the entire Middle School team. You are the only person involved in this process that did not share the goal of getting Lawrence through 8th grade...

...What is most painful to me is that Lawrence doesn't understand why you did not communicate your decision to her. She initiated her personal appeal to you and had full faith in you to help her reach her goal of completing Middle School. She has learned a lot in this matter and unfortunately she now doubts the integrity of authority due to the way you handled this. In her words she said "Dad, where are the checks and balances?" "How does one person get to do this?" You should be proud of Lawrence, she initially approached you on this matter and she communicated effectively with you. You, on the other hand, dismissed her with a letter. Your exercise of your authority needs to be examined, and I am confident that is happening now...

Yesterday you blocked my family's access to the school website. What is up with that? I guess this is the added insult to injury part. My family has 3 graduates and we no longer have access to the website? Amazing...

Dickson never responded and we continued our search for a new school for Lawrence.

To this day Doug does not receive any correspondence
from this institution his Alma mater.

CHAPTER 23
Family Loyalty

A S WE CONTINUED TO TALK to and interview with other schools it became evident Lawrence had only one local private school choice. One of Bailey's high school teachers recommended we consider an all girl's boarding school with equestrian riding in another state. Doug and Lawrence were apprehensive at the thought of her leaving while I thought it could be a good idea. Lawrence ruled out the one local private school that would admit her at this late date and Doug and I did not feel comfortable forcing a school on her. Two medical professionals advised us that Lawrence viewing her peers on a constant basis would be an incessant and negative reminder of her unnecessary dismissal which could prove detrimental to her emotionally and academically. Doug and I analyzed the pros and cons of sending her and what would be the most beneficial to her under the adverse and unfair circumstances she has fallen victim to.

We anxiously waited to find out if she would be accepted to the boarding school. Their deadline for acceptance was April 1st, so we knew it was a huge accommodation to consider admitting a new student weeks before the start of school. Lawrence was warming up to the thought of a new environment and the opportunity to reinvent herself while regaining her self-esteem. We found ourselves in the most difficult situation due to the entire disruption caused by one man's abrupt decision. The miscalculations of her grades were a human mistake, but not admitting his responsibility while exerting his power was both unjust and cruel to the seventh grade girl.

It was true that Lawrence had missed Dickson's artificial criteria by one point, and she had been on academic warning for two consecutive semesters. It was also true that she had begun owning her academic success and failures and had committed herself to do what was necessary to finish Middle School. In addition, she had made a personal appeal in April to Headmaster Short, who suggested she should drop her most difficult course, Spanish, and replace it with Latin in the upcoming fall. Lawrence welcomed the idea of getting out of Spanish as she was having a hard time mastering the subject. I was grateful for the efforts from principal David Jacobs and vice principal Cindy Heard, who truly attempted to see Lawrence achieve the goal of getting our child through the eight-grade.

Doug and I were terrible anxious over our daughter not being enrolled in school for the fall. We also worried about the possibility of sending her far away. We had never taken a child away to school and Doug was opposed to the idea the entire time. The thought of "sending my baby away" caused a profound hurt to the core of my soul. I was confident God would protect her and guide her, but my unwillingness to give up control would be my greatest challenge. I knew I had to let this go because I was the one who had promoted boarding school as the best available option.

Lawrence's sixth year at summer camp was approaching and she was looking forward to reuniting with her many camp companions who lived all over the state. The upcoming two-week adventure to the beautiful Texas Hill Country was several weeks away when suddenly we realized an unexpected calendar conflict. If Lawrence were to be accepted she would have to report to school during the last week of camp.

Once again our nervous tension level was building as we had to make a difficult decision whether or not to place Lawrence on the bus for camp departure. At that point she had not been accepted to school and camp was a family tradition; Doug attended this camp as a child as did Bailey and Jay. We knew if she gained acceptance to the boarding school we would have to retrieve her one-week early from camp having paid the full tuition. We decided it was best to forego camp, and Lawrence was very mature handling the decision. She viewed boarding school as the best option and was hoping she would be accepted within the next few days. Not attending summer camp was another disappointment, but we were proud of her positive outlook in pursuit of her new academic path.

Lawrence nervously awaited the school's decision and was ready to put her departure into motion. The logistics of getting all this done stressed me out and trying to cope with the concept of becoming an empty nester before my time made it worse. With each day the uncertainty unsettled our lives. I constantly reminded myself to break it down into "Baby Steps" and "Take it One Day at a Time." This was good in theory but difficult to practice. I couldn't focus on anything other than my daughter's dismissal and the fact she had not been in school for six weeks. I knew middle school was a formative time and their official grades were not listed on transcripts. It was time for me to cut some ties in Lawrence's academic life and if that resulted in some failures, this was an opportune time for her to experience it. High school was one year away, and I knew my child had to accept her educational challenges and acknowledge that several hurdles must be overcome to achieve success.

A wise Christian woman, Christina Harper, once said to a bible study group I was a part of many years ago, with regards to her grown children: "I will not accept responsibility for their successes, nor will I accept responsibilities for their failures." I didn't understand this statement when I first heard it but I understand it now. These words are what I had strived for as a mother. I must teach, guide, and lead them but the most important thing I can do for my children is to instill in them an independence that will hopefully motivate them and give them the tools to be successful. Only God's hand can enable me to release my children from my control. My head was telling me to let Lawrence go; my heart was not on board. If she were accepted I would take that as a sign to let her go and find her way. The pain of disrespect and mistreatment from our Headmaster Dickson Short may never go away, but now it was time to forget the Hurt and make the most of this very difficult situation for our daughter. However; my baby being seven hours away would be painful, we must trust that it would be the right decision.

Lawrence's acceptance to the all Girls - Catholic boarding school came one week later from the Admission's Director and confirmed with a phone call and a few days later with a letter in the mail. Our family was thrilled for Lawrence to be given this opportunity as I found myself entering "It's Business" mode mindset to prepare for her departure in three days. Lawrence and I headed to Dallas to shop for bedding essentials and the equestrian store for the many essentials for the upcoming school year. She was excited that she could take her horse with her and this was the motivation factor in her decision to choose an equestrian boarding school over the limited option she had at home. She was apprehensive about not having everything she needed, but I reassured her we could send her whatever she needed. Clothes, bedding and personal products were on the top of our list with books and uniforms completed during orientation. It was invigorating to have a new challenge in our lives and knowing we had a plan was encouraging.

Word of her acceptance spread quickly and several of her friends planned a "surprise" going away party within those few days. I told Lawrence we were having dinner with two families to celebrate her acceptance as a ruse, only to surprise her with thirty of her friends for a pizza/swim party. She was touched by her friend's expression with the party while her pending departure and new school home had not been completely comprehended. None of the kids left without giving Lawrence a hug. Some gave words of encouragement; some expressed feelings of anger over the circumstances and all displayed a genuine love for my daughter.

Our Saturday departure got off to a slow start, which caused a late arrival for our overnight stay at the nearby hotel. The next morning brought hot coffee and a scenic drive through long, winding country roads leading to the historic campus, surrounded by the many old, beautiful oak trees. The school was found in 1821 and has continually operated to this day. We were all a little nervous about the unfamiliar surroundings, but were somewhat excited about being at such an established place in a different part of the country. The enrollment new admissions process was time consuming and tedious, but we passed the time eaves dropping on the many Spanish speaking families that predominated the new students. The orientation started at ten o'clock sharp and the eight-hour day consisted of several meetings, dorm move in, and lunch with our new school community. Every family had an interesting story that brought their daughter to this school and it was apparent the girls came from diverse backgrounds and would discover many new things through their new experiences together.

The day was overwhelming with all the new information, and regulations. A few minutes before the entire student body and families were to convene for the welcome mass I experienced an overwhelming wave of emotion. The tears began to flow as I suddenly realized I was about to leave my daughter at a school hundreds of miles away from home. I was completely beside myself. During the orientation Mass I was unable to control my emotions. The front of my shirt turned a different color from the soil of my tears. Lawrence, Doug and I all agreed that boarding school was the right choice, but it wasn't until that exact moment that I was actually realizing in my heart that we were leaving her at this strange place. Lawrence starting pleading not to leave her in this unknown school as it suddenly had me gasping for air. "Don't leave me here, I will do better," she begged. "Please take me home with you" she whispered over and over during the service. It was as if I was in a dream and having no idea where I was or who these people were. My mind was in a fog and my heart devastated for the upcoming good-bye. I knew when it was time to leave her and it needed to be fast; immediately after the Mass. At the conclusion of the welcome celebration, I turned to Doug and anxiously told him I would not be able to attend the post service reception. I had to get out of there quickly so right after the Mass we went back to Lawrence's newly decorated room for our final goodbyes.

The walk back to her dorm felt as if it was miles away. The winding path between each building reminded me of the long and never ending yellow brick road. The three of us entered her dorm room and I reached towards my child for one last embrace.

As I hugged my baby I told her how much I loved her and reminded her why we were taking this aggressive step. "You know this is for your academic success," I reminded her while at the same time reassuring myself. "You have to figure out your schooling and at the end of the day you must get through the system with achievement." I was crying uncontrollably, "You don't want to be me, 47 years old with a family, full-time job and working towards your undergraduate degree." Lawrence and Doug were sobbing as our departure was imminent. We embraced in a tight hug as her tears dripped down my back. It was a special and most emotional moment. Lawrence had resigned herself that she was going to be a boarding school student and to a certain extent handled the emotion of the moment better than her parents.

Lawrence taught me so much that day. My thirteen-year-old had such a loving and mature heart. Here was a child coping with the deaths of two family members with whom she was extremely close to and now she was faced with a life separated from her family and friends. She was finding her way academically and taking ownership in her work. She wasn't solely responsible for her academic challenges. I should have stayed on her more; I should have participated more in her homework and monitored her grades more closely. If there was ever a time to give someone some slack due to adverse circumstances Lawrence had earned that right, but instead her life seemed to get more difficult at every turn. She is a wonderful child and as painful as it was Lawrence grew from these experiences and it made her stronger. One month prior to her dismissal she was given the Middle School citizenship award at the spring choral performance.

After our long hug, I stepped aside for Doug to start his goodbye. I was somewhat at a loss for words and the thought of leaving her standing all alone in the stark dorm room caused a pit in my stomach. I quickly went into her new suitemate's room and motioned to the three girls to come to our rescue. "Please go be with Lawrence" I tearfully whimpered. The girls realizing the emotions of the moment leaped to their feet and within seconds were hugging their new friend. It was a touching scene and as I motioned to Doug that the time was right to depart and without words spoken we jumped in to the car and drove fifty miles north in complete silence with tears rolling down our faces.

As the sky darkened we decided to spend the night in the next town because the stress and emotion had drained us.We picked up dinner to go and after unloading the car for the fourth time in forty-eight hours, I hung our clothes in the closet and immediately took to the bed.

We took our time leaving the sleepy town the next morning, unmotivated and sad as we realized we had no one to go home to. We were emotionally and physically exhausted that bordered on depression. We arrived back in Fort Worth early afternoon. We were finally home and I once again took to the bed.

My Baby is Gone

My heart is aching for a bully's rule
it was so unnecessary and very cruel
she is missing her family and many of her friends
she is asking already to come to visit for a long weekend

*trustee's said their hands were tied and the
Emperor's rule had full command
a true group people holds accountable the acts
and consequences of an egotistical man
our summer was ruined with an unexpected school search
trips and summer camp were canceled with the
combination on being left in the lurch
I struggle with so many things and not sure
where to place it in my mind
I really want to be sweet but with everything that has happened
it makes me feel so helpless and unkind.
I need to feel God's arms around me and his true loving grace
at this time my heart is overwhelmed and in a very difficult place*

The next day Doug was moving slowly to the shower as I announced my sudden decision to take a "mental health" day. I wanted to lie in my bed and stay in my home by myself to reflect on the events of the last two months. I was still at a loss as to why this whole situation transpired with the hope that Dickson would realize the consequences of an impulsive decision. Just like the emperor who ruled with a heavy hand and one day naked as he addressed his kingdom. In the mind of a bully their word is law and any questioning of challenging of authority brings a swift and aggressive response. Bullies thrive by staying on offense and are very uncomfortable on defense.

My expectations for others were high and this is where I went wrong. Expectations are everything. I hoped Lawrence would be reinstated, but when that proved not possible then it was our hope to salvage our forty-three year history with the school by receiving an apology from Dickson for the way he handled the situation. Doug and I felt passionately about the unspoken "Family Loyalty" law and had hoped others would display empathy to our family during this disruptive time. In my opinion the school's policy of granting such absolute power to one person should be reviewed and amended to prevent the mistreatment we experienced. We were hopeful that certain members of the Board of Trustees would stand up to Dickson and right the wrong he created. We will never know what the Board said to Dickson, but we do know he was reprimanded which gave rise to his vindictiveness. The ability to appeal our case to the Executive Committee of the Board requesting reinstatement would have been a logical and fair process, but school policy does not allow for that. The arbitrary grade point criterion established by Headmaster Short couple with his dishonesty and disrespect warranted a review of his decision. Additionally, the way we were treated added insult to injury. We had invested over 120k in this school and our daughter's education as she was dismissed over one point. We were not the only victims here; Dickson also bullied his staff to protect his position and ego. My theory was confirmed, when he locked Doug, Bailey and Jay from the school's website as graduating alumni. Once again, he was exercising his strength and authority in an unethical way.

Just because you can doesn't necessarily mean you should!

Returning to work the following day was a tall task. I knew it was a good thing I had something to get me out of bed because "Debbie Downer" was taking over my head. I could feel her presence in every thought. When suddenly I received a phone call from another parent asking me aggressively "when" and "if" my husband and I were going to get past this situation? I was so caught off guard by her insensitivity that I burst into tears. I gasped for breaths for the next word and said, "I just took my baby seven hours away to a school I know nothing about and where we do not know one person. We will get over this, but it will be on our time." Within seconds the conversation turned aggressive. "How dare you say that to me?" I firmly stated. She immediately reiterated, "You both just have to move on." The conversation turned hostile, as I immediately stated, "It's not enough anymore to pay tuition and give to the annual fund," I said. "Since we were not big donors, we were treated with disrespect." With emotions high, she immediately disagreed with my contention. "Don't insult me," I said. "I do this for a living, I know how this works." Suddenly, there was a moment of silence. "You are right" she said. "That is how it works." With nothing else to say the conversation came to a close.

I was devastated and completely distraught. I picked up my gym bag and headed for the recreation center. I hurriedly put on my workout clothes and landed on the treadmill. Lawrence's God Mother casually called me on my cell phone and again I burst into tears and cried out for my baby's departure. I sobbed while trying to balance on the moving belt for the unfair treatment from yet another bully. The disrespect of a man's actions towards my husband and family was not my main concern, but the lasting consequences of how his actions could affect my daughter's emotional well-being in the years to come.

I contained my nervous breakdown, returned back to the office and decided to plunge into my work and redirected my focus. An hour later while sitting at my desk I answered a phone call from my mother. I nonchalantly picked up the receiver to hear my mother's distraught voice. She was crying out in a deep despair, "Steve is dead, Steve is dead! They found your brother dead in his apartment."

Within seconds my world came to another screeching halt and my breathing suddenly stopped as time stood still. My mind couldn't process the traumatic news. The loss of another sibling was too much to handle. I was preoccupied by Lawrence's situation and now I was dealt with something far more serious. My bad day had just gotten worse, as my concerns immediately turned to my mother who had just lost her second child in eighteen months.

Chapter 24
Emotionally Unstable

TIME STOOD STILL AND WITHIN seconds my world went from bad to worse. I remember the shock and my frozen mannequin pose. Mother was unable to control her emotions and I could feel her turmoil with every word.

I was speechless as I asked for her permission to gather my thoughts and call her back. My heart was crashing to the floor. How could this be happening again to our family? I couldn't believe Terry and Mrs. Woodson were gone, but now my baby brother? It was a challenge for me to have even an encouraging thought. I felt defeated with complete hopelessness. I was barely comprehending the other two deaths and now adding Steve to their selected company was unthinkable. I knew in my heart they were with their Maker, but trying to convince my mind was inconceivable.

I had so many feelings to overcome, and I knew how important it was to keep moving forward. For I was fearful if I stopped, I may not be able to start again.

My injured arm was becoming heavier with each step and my strides were becoming more labored. The pain from the broken bone was a full reality as the agonizing pain was radiating to my brain.

I wanted to stop and cry out for help, but I could hear a little voice in my head encouraging me to move towards the finish line. The cheers from the crowd had faded into the distance, and with little effort or desire I could feel my exhaustion taking over my body. I was injured and I wanted to quit. Tears were building in each eye and with each blink; the wind gush interrupting their streamline flow and I could taste the salty tears in my mouth.

A few minutes later my state of shock diminished and I regained some emotional stability. I gathered my thoughts picked up the phone to inform Doug of Steve's sudden death. Before I could give him the news, he sadly whimpered he was having a bad day with Lawrence being gone and it was preoccupying his thoughts. I informed him that his day was about to get worse as I shared with him the sudden death of my baby brother.

There were few words to say amongst family members now faced with the tragedy of another departed member. Disbelief and sadness overwhelmed us all as the harsh reality began to set in. My family of eight children had now been whittled to six, and the immensity of this event was inconceivable. My siblings and I found ourselves once again in the parenting role, as the details and logistics of another funeral fell upon us. Our life was a nightmare that was never ending. Lawrence was no longer under our roof and my family had lost a third loved one. It was so heart breaking, so once again I shifted into "It's Business" mode and pressed forward. This time I was familiar with the process and coached myself to keep moving forward. I now understood my emotional capabilities and limitations. Frankly, I didn't have the strength to host another funeral, as I was drained and exhausted from Lawrence's abrupt departure.

The next few days were the hardest as news of Steve's death spread amongst family and friends. It was a unanimous family decision to hold the service in the town that we all called home Memphis, Tennessee. We had moved from Memphis to Oklahoma City thirty-years ago, but always considered ourselves Memphians. With the help of family and friends, we were able to return to our hometown community to say goodbye to one of our very own. It was a precious time for our family as we gathered to remember a funny guy with a heart that was larger than life. Steve lived life to its full capacity and it was not a secret that a healthy life style was not his top priority. He lived in Los Angeles for years trying to break into the entertainment and film industry as that was his passion. He was a comedian by nature and his impressions of many celebrities were exceptional and often brought life to a dull party. He had developed friendship with talent agent Jay Bernstein and through his connections Steve appeared in multiple episodes of *Seinfeld* and *Becker*. Our family of eight children had reduced to six in eighteen months. This was another sad time in our lives and we knew God's love and guidance would eventually heal our aching hearts. We received so much love and support from our extended family and friends as that enabled us to endure another tragedy.

Why was this happening? My life was being dominated by disappointment and sadness due to a permanent loss of three family members and the temporary loss of my baby girl. I knew God had his hand in all of this, but my strong, impatient nature caused me to question myself and the strength. My sanity and exhaustion level increased daily with each hurdle, but I knew I couldn't quit now with graduation in sight. It was refreshing to imagine a less stressful life. I was starting to question everything in my life and its purpose.

Momentum

I am starting to lose momentum with my mind and body taking toll
I am feeling a deep sadness down to the bottom of my soul
the overall work and school experience has been a true gift from above
I will be able to leave the legacy of learning to my children with love
I am starting to question my life at this fast rapid pace
as I know I must stay focused on the goal and finish the race

Through my family's three deaths, I had come to realize the pain we experience from their loss is really for ourselves. Those of us left behind are the ones in the emotional pain, the departed are the lucky ones. The departed are with their Maker. Terry, Jo Ann and Steve are with the Lord in a perfect existence. I knew this in my mind, but my heart felt differently.

"For the LORD is good; his mercy is everlasting;
and his truth endured to all generations."
Psalm 100:5

Lawrence was in her first week of boarding school and the stress of being away from her family and friends was starting to make her homesick. We had made arrangements for her horse to be shipped to the boarding school, but the timing of his arrival was delayed by two weeks due to scheduling.

Doug and I struggled with how to break the news of Steve's death to Lawrence and reluctantly decided to postpone telling her since her new school experience had just started. Through email to multiple friends, I requested they ask their children not mention my brother's death to Lawrence through emails or text messaging. However, she received a message from a friend expressing her sympathy of her Uncle's passing. Lawrence immediately picked up the phone and called my mother in Oklahoma City. She tearfully asked my mother if the information was true and when the funeral would be. It was proving to be a challenge to arrange a flight for her due to the remote location of the campus, transportation to and from the airport along with the additional expense. Because school had been in session for only three days missing four days of classes would immediately place Lawrence in a bind to catch up.

Bailey and Jay were Rush Chairmen of their sorority and fraternity and leaving town during the week was problematic due to the timing. Doug and I decided to maintain our children's schedules and responsibilities so just the two of us attended Steve's funeral in Memphis. We had not yet recovered from the emotional exhaustion from the taking of Lawrence to boarding school, and the first week of being empty nesters was most depressing.

CHAPTER 25
Never Say Never

L IFE WITH LAWRENCE GONE WAS an adjustment, but knowing she was safe, made it manageable. Each day we waited for her nightly phone call with the details of her day. One night we received a panicked phone call informing us of a hurricane headed straight for the campus. Doug and I just shook our heads in disbelief with another drama, but confident the school would be prepared due to their experiences. They made the decision to evacuate the boarding students transporting the girls thirteen hours inland via an un-air-conditioned school bus. Doug and I were concerned about them departing the campus in the middle of the night and later found out the reason was due to the heat which did make sense. Lawrence stayed in constant communication with us during the evacuation, and the thought of her on a school bus with no seat belts in bumper-to-bumper traffic had us up most of the night worrying about their journey. The main highway leading out of harm's way was log jammed as thousands of coastal residents moved inland. It made us a nervous wreck to visualize of our baby in an uncomfortable school bus in the middle of the night, but once again, we had no control over the situation so we said a prayer and waited for the next phone call.

Time was of the essence due to the speed of the storm so transporting Lawrence's horse to a safer location was out of the question without enough time and man power the trainer chose to stay with the thirty horses under her direction so they could hopefully be returned after the storm. In emergency situations such as this all the horses are turned out to pasture with gates open to give them a better chance of survival.

Lawrence was upset to leave her best friend behind, but obeyed her superiors as she said what she hoped would not be her last good-bye before stepping onto the bus. I told myself if something happens to that horse, I would take it as a sign to throw in the towel and bring her home.

The stress and emotion of this latest situation consumed me. Doug and I were baffled as to why all this drama and tension was continuing. My husband remained calm and upbeat but I was at wits end being the "scary cat" I am over violent weather.

As the bus arrived at its destination in the early morning hours a phone call from Lawrence brought me a deep sigh of relief. Work that day was a challenge due to sleep deprivation and distractions caused by fellow employees who had heard the news of the evacuation.

The hurricane ripped through the campus in a horrific way. High winds spawned multiple twisters that damaged the campus and buildings to the school for weeks. The small town community came together to assist the school in clearing one hundred year old trees had been uprooted like yard weeds making many of the rural roads impassable. Chain saws were the most sought after piece of equipment.

As the clean-up continued 500 miles away from the boarding school, the girls bunked together in an Austin dorm. Lawrence with five mates found her space sleeping in a closet and was calling home regularly giving us updates. After a couple days we realized the bus was not heading back to campus anytime soon, so I decided to drive to Austin to be with my baby.

We gathered her belongings and headed for a family friend's home on the lake. It was such a wonderful three days with Lawrence as we ate at her favorite restaurants and attended a local spa. My niece, Cary joined us and Lawrence promptly enlisted her in the campaign to bring Lawrence home. Cary was a school teacher and each day, Lawrence would beg me to take her home and enroll her in the public school. It was painful to listen to her many appeals to return home, and I constantly reminded her of our one-year commitment.

We had a wonderful time together cruising around town and doing the girl thing. She continually pleaded with me to bring her take her back to Fort Worth as the presence of another hurricane was gaining strength in the Gulf fueled her argument. Doug and I were hesitant to bring her back for fear that she would not want to return. Lawrence's mood deteriorated throughout the days as the "homesickness" element was in full force. She was tired and yearned for her own bed, not to mention her lifelong friends.

Our last night together in Austin was a sad one. Throughout the night, Lawrence persisted about going home which was painful. When I gave her the final no, she cried herself to sleep. It saddened me that I must return her back to her new school, but I needed to return to work and she needed to get back to her academics. Be that as I may I was so torn by this continuing and difficult saga.

The Struggle is Back

I am leaving her tomorrow
My heart is broken in two
I am feeling so guilty and a failure as a mother too
she will be heading back down that highway for another thirteen hours
I will be so nervous for her safety, as I am becoming very sour
she cried all night begging me to take her back home
she pledged her wiliness to accomplish her
schoolwork in a very loving tone
I am questioning our decision on sending her back to this school
why has this happened to my daughter, I feel like such a fool

October 13, 2008

The following day I received a phone call from the boarding school mom to meet at the bus within the hour. With the second hurricane heading toward the campus, it was decided for the bus to return to the town nearest the school and disperse the boarders to local families to ensure their safety. Doug and I were not comfortable with Lawrence relocating to another unfamiliar place and immediately suggested that I bring her back home and he would drive her back after the second hurricane passed. The campus did not have full power and with another storm on its way a return to normal did not seem imminent.

Lawrence was going on her second week of missed classes and Doug and I were concerned about all her make-up work. Besides the actual schoolwork, the boarding school had requested additional testing in the nearby town accessing her learning abilities by our previous school. Her previous testing period had expired for more than a year and according to the boarding school, it was the responsibility of her previous school to notify us of the lapse documentation.

According to our previous school, she had multiple learning disabilities and qualified for additional test taking time. The new testing required by the boarding school was an additional $1200 commitment and was requirement upon her acceptance to the school. The three testing sessions were interrupted by the storms ripping through the area, but would resume when she returned to campus.

During the week of Lawrence's brief arrival, she chose not to reveal to any of her old friends of her homecoming by attending her old school and surprising her old friends. As she approached the Friday night game, she suddenly became mauled by her old classmates and as immediate body dog pile of students instantly formed on the ground near the football field.

The following Monday, Doug enrolled her in the public school system for the next five days. Once again Lawrence found herself in a new academic environment.

The second hurricane did not cause additional damage to the campus and within a few days the school was open for business. There were ripped tiles hanging from the ceilings, broken trees, and leaky floors but the 200 year structure remained in tack and ready for the students.

Lawrence's week was considered a success in the public school and our worst fear of Lawrence not wanting to return to the boarding school was coming true. She was continuing stating her case on why she should not return, but Doug and I felt firm on her returning to the school and completing the 8th grade year. This poor child has been through the emotional and physical ringer. She has been passed around from school to school and shuffled in and out of unfamiliar towns.

Following Lawrence's second departure the next few days were filled with sadness once again. Doug and I found ourselves missing Lawrence even more the second time since she had been sleeping in her bed for the past week. My workload was at a full capacity in the office, but my focus centered on securing my undergraduate degree. My goal was truly in sight at this point. I resigned myself to not allow the sadness or distractions knock me off course and completing my last six hours of school.

Later that week three of my close friends organized an impromptu cocktail hour that turned into a "Bring Lawrence Home Campaign." I was taken by surprise their suggestion of pulling her out of the boarding school initially I didn't know how to respond. What kind of example would we set quitting? My sadness turned emotional as I grew defensive probably due to guilt that Doug and I had made a mistake as the logic of their words sunk in. Two sips into my first cocktail, I burst into tears. My friends meant well in offering their unsolicited opinions, but they didn't detect my fragile state of mind. In my spontaneous breakdown they came to realize the emotional toll all the hurdles had taken on me and for the first time, I was offered the opportunity to surrender to the drama.

Intervention

The ladies came together to help me understand
my life is way too full like a bucket of sand
bring Lawrence home they said she is starting to have a fit
the three women stood together to convince me to quit
I just want my family to be together again with little drama in the end
I listened to the girl's advice because I trust them as loyal friends
"My Friends are My Family" and I have
once again reminded this is true
they are constantly recuing me from a crisis and lifting me up too

A month later Doug traveled to the out of state campus to attend the traditional Father/Daughter dinner dance. He was excited about the long weekend with Lawrence and the opportunity to meet her new friends and teachers, but had some concern relative to an incident on a field trip. Doug left in the early morning hours that Friday to make a meeting with the Headmistress he requested to address the troubling incident involving Lawrence a week or two prior. Since the boarding school was in a remote area they would regularly take all the boarders by bus to the nearest town about thirty minutes away. The girls looked forward to these field trips where they could browse the mall shops, take in a movie and go out to eat. The eating out often took center stage for most of the girls who didn't care for the typical cafeteria style school food. Lawrence's favorite was a locally famous fried chicken restaurant that she said "makes the best chicken in the world." On the night of the incident all the girls dined together at a mall restaurant and were then offered the choice of shopping or returning to the bus to wait for the field trip to end and head back to campus. Lawrence and a friend returned to the bus having already spent their allowance money which the school would collect from the parents monthly and dole out to the girls for the field trips. One of the regular bus drivers employed by the boarding school solely for this purpose opened the door and the girls proceeded to the rear to listen to their music and "chill out" as they call it when suddenly someone in full Halloween costume approached the rear window of the bus and asked the girls to open the window. With no suspicions Lawrence's friend opened the window and the masked man asked the girls if they wanted to get off the bus and "hang out." At that point the girls sensed some creepiness and kiddingly told the guy to get lost as they closed the window. They reinserted their ear buds and turned up the volume thinking he would go away, but moments later looked up to see him standing inside the bus walkway a couple seats away from where they were seated. The experienced bus driver had let him onto the bus by telling him he was a friend of the girls. Taken by surprise both girls leaped to their feet to exit the bus, but he sat down and lifted his leg across the aisle to block their way as the driver was preoccupied with his nose in a newspaper. The masked man told the girls to remain quiet as he placed his hand on the friend's thigh. From her cell phone Lawrence quickly dialed the boarding school "Mom" who was inside the mall and calmly told her there was a problem at the bus. The man was focused on Lawrence's friend and didn't realize she had made the call until she had communicated the situation. The school Mom immediately sprinted across the mall parking lot, entered the bus, confronted the intruder and harshly reprimanded the driver for letting the man onto the bus. Right after making that phone call Lawrence frantically called Doug who was at a football game so he couldn't hear her clearly, but could tell something was wrong. Lawrence texted both of us expressing her fear over the situation. Once Doug exited the stadium he immediately called the boarding school Mom having left the game early and she verified that there was a situation and everything was under control. Doug demanded specific details and she confirmed his suspicions that a serious error in judgment had occurred at which point he laid into her. The next day she summoned Lawrence to her room at the front of the residence hall and aggressively told Lawrence she was never in any danger and that she didn't appreciate her calling us about the incident. Immediately after the meeting, Lawrence called us in tears and that verified in our minds that not only was the issue significant, but that the school Mom felt compelled to intimidate our daughter as damage control. I was upset, but Doug was beside himself to the point that I had to convince him that it didn't make sense for him to go to the school the next day. We were focused on Lawrence's adjustment in an unfamiliar environment and never contemplated her personal safety would be an issue as we took it for granted at a one hundred plus year old all girls school. What a flawed assumption that turned out to be.

Doug entered the spacious and historic office of the Headmistress which was located at the front of the beautiful campus, and she cordially welcomed him and thanked him for traveling to attend the dinner/dance. He had scripted in his mind what he planned to say, but was immediately knocked off course when she expressed concern over the event without admitting blame and told Doug that the bus driver had been admonished and reassigned to another position. Accepting the words of the leader of the school Doug abandoned his script and withheld all the comments he had rehearsed in his mind during the long drive. The Headmistress then took control of the conversation by telling Doug she was concerned with Lawrence's behavior and her seemingly unwillingness to adjust to the school's processes and procedures. While Lawrence always struggled in the classroom, never once was she ever cited for misbehavior or a poor attitude. The Headmistress then told Doug that their time was up, and that she wanted to reconvene after lunch with Lawrence, the dorm Mom to close the loop on the Halloween event and address the other issues. Doug viewed this as a good thing even though he knew it would put Lawrence in an awkward position.

Doug thanked the Headmistress for her time and asked how to find Lawrence. Third period was near conclusion and she suggested he wait outside the main building adjacent to the office. The bell rang and a sea of uniformed girls exited as Doug stayed out of the way trying to find Lawrence. Minutes later she emerged and Doug immediately approached her with excitement, but Lawrence didn't share her father's emotion. Clearly she was stressed and asked him to calm down and they went around the corner to talk. Doug remained positive despite the cold reception and told Lawrence that his meeting with the Headmistress went well and that he felt much better about her being here. He went on to tell her what the Headmistress said about the incident specifically that she said the bus driver was punished and is no longer a bus driver. Lawrence looked at her father in disbelief and told him that the bus driver took them on their field trip a couple days ago and was just recognized at Friday Mass for his many years of service.

Needless to say Doug was confused and suspicious, but didn't reveal what he had just learned when the group meeting started. The Headmistress initiated the conversation by telling Doug that she was mistaken and that the bus driver was not reassigned and apologized for indicating otherwise. Doug reiterated his concerns and the Headmistress promptly redirected the conversation towards Lawrence not accepting proper procedure and respecting authority. Doug yielded to the comments without confrontation allowing them to say what they wanted to say. This meeting was hard on Lawrence, and I know Doug would have preferred to let them know what he really thought, but I was proud of him for his discretion.

The Friday night dinner/dance was fun for both father and daughter although Lawrence didn't want to stay as long as Doug did so they left early and headed to the nearby town where Doug had reserved a room. The following day, a football showdown between two rival southeast conference schools was about to take place and Doug being such a huge college football fan was determined to travel another hour to experience the big game. My father/daughter duo had a wonderful Saturday experiencing the largest tailgate party they had ever seen and a game that went to double overtime and as they walked hand in hand to the remote parking lot which was actually a family's backyard they realized it was almost time to once again to say goodbye and return to the daily routine we all had come to hate.

Doug had trouble sleeping that night as he struggled with our decision to send Lawrence to boarding school coupled with her homesickness and the recent disturbing event. Throughout the weekend Lawrence repeatedly expressed her desire to return home which weighed heavy on Doug's mind. My husband has always resisted change as it makes him feel uncomfortable, but once a change is made he always resigns himself to stay the course despite adversity so now that we were in this position he was reluctant to remove Lawrence from the school. He went to sleep that night believing the best course of action was to encourage Lawrence to stay the course, but awoke the next day feeling otherwise. He immediately called home in an emotional moment telling me he had a change of heart and wanted to bring Lawrence home. "What has happened to our life," he asked me and "how did Lawrence end up at boarding school?" I was taken aback by his sudden change of heart, but knew I must defer to him because he was there and I was not. While we were on the phone Doug spotted the principal of the school in the distance riding a lawnmower and I encouraged him to approach her to share his thoughts. He hung up the phone and they had a heart to heart conversation regarding Doug's concern for his daughter's safety as well as her emotional well-being with all the events from the last four months. Two hours later, I received a phone call from the principal informing me of Lawrence's departure with her father. Your husband was "precious" she said; I have never seen a grown man cry before. "Lawrence is a wonderful child and her father is a caring man" she stated and I hate to see her leave, but I now understand why she needs to be home with her family.

I was shocked as I immediately came to grips with the fact that Lawrence was coming home and I had much to do to prepare for her arrival. Within minutes, my father/daughter team called me announcing the spontaneous decision and that Lawrence had packed up all her belongings in less than twenty minutes. Lawrence said when she looked up and saw her daddy come back for her it was the happiest moment in her life!

CHAPTER 26
Red Shoes

SOME WILL VIEW MY JOURNEY as a long road trip wrought with detours and winding roads; others will see a complete train wreck. My adventure was long and exhausting and it continues to this day, but as this portion of my life's journal comes to a close I see things in a different light, a more beautiful light; perhaps one that I never imagined. I find myself viewing the many beautiful colors over the rainbow as if I were looking through the sheer lens of a kaleidoscope. The many shades of color remind me of the "hurdles" in my life. The multiple tinted lenses represent the wisdom I have acquired through life's unexpected drama. As with most journeys the road was not familiar and the obstacles unexpected and I feared I would not reach my destination. There were several times the road was not familiar and I was fearful my travels would be unsuccessful. However, through the love and guidance of my family and friends, my travel remained on course and my determination continued.

The truth is I have matured more over the last five years than in the previous forty-nine. I truly believe God has been with me in my journey and for the first time in my life I have allowed Him to navigate my path with less resistance. My husband has kept me centered and by example taught me more than any teacher. I have learned much from my children; perhaps as much as they have learned from me.

My predicament was similar to Dorothy's in the *Wizard of Oz*. Dorothy could have gone home at any time, but she didn't realize it as she insisted on doing things her way. Instead of asking the right questions and trusting herself she chose a long, yellow brick road that contained many unexpected hurdles.

So many times we strive to leave our family's physical existence, only to spend our entire life returning to our place of origin. Who we are is where we have come from. Many of us spend our adult life fighting or denying that journey. Good or bad, our experiences influence our decisions which ultimately comprise our existence. We bring on our journey our confidence, struggles and dysfunctions. Every family has some form of dysfunction except for Ward and June Cleaver. With courage, strength and heart we can always find our way back to the road of success.

I found my way at the end of my rainbow although I was slow to recognize the dysfunction that unknowingly had held me back for a long time. It has been revealed to me that I can be successful through my experiences, many blessings through the love of my family and friends. Glenda, the Good Witch of the East (my mother) prepared me for my journey with hope and encouragement. She gave me a pair of ruby red slippers (God's love and eternal salvation) as my protection for the long journey (life). The Wicked Witch of the West (my "hurdles") wreaked havoc with my confidence, but the Land of the Munchkins (my friends) always offered unconditional love and support. The Wizard of Oz (Doug) motivated and encouraged me to pursue my dream (my degree).

My children have mirrored their gifts to me during this journey. God lent me these individuals to nurture and love, as I know one day they will be returned. The thought of losing a child is a difficult concept to grasp. However, I know with God's love the loss will be painful but can be endured. I have felt many times over the years that I must be on a completely different time table than my Maker. I have come to learn, I am on the same time table I just didn't realize there was a time difference.

The Scarecrow (Lawrence) has the brains and "street smarts" of us all. She communicates her well thought words and that is often revealed to me through her ability to see one's true character. She may be on her own time table with her learning, but in the end will prevail and cause embarrassment to those who did not allow her the opportunity to continue her course. I was amazed to receive a copy of an e-mail

Lawrence had sent to Dickson while she was at boarding school after learning of his illness.

From: Lawrence
To: Dickson, Short
Sent: Sat, 18 Oct 2008
Mr. Short -
I have recently been told about your illness and I just wanted to let you know that my family and I are very sorry to hear about it. I have heard from several different people that the treatment is going better than they had expected. It seems like the Woodson family aren't the only family with enough obstacles to handle for the year. I hope that you get well soon.
Sincerely,
Lawrence Woodson

From: Dickson, Short
To: Lawrence
Sent: Sat, 18 Oct 2008 9:39 am
Subject: Re:
L
Thanks.
Remember, God gives us only that which we can handle!
Hope you're having a good year!
Mr. S

(sic)
From: Lawrence
To: short@dicksonps.org
Sent: Sat, 18 Oct 2008
Subject: (no subject)
Mr. Short,
Yes. It is very true that he will only give us what we can handle, but I always like to think we have control over our own situations. The year has been rough but my whole situation is out of my hands. I hope you feel better.
Lawrence

The Tin Man (Bailey) has displayed her loving heart time and time again. She continues to love me through all my dysfunctional "mother" moments, and she has helped me become a more loving and patient woman. She has taught me the heart must guide our decisions with unconditional love at all times.

The Lion (Jay) has revealed to me that courage is a required trait to be successful. Jay's confidence and positive attitude have demonstrated his true character and had a tremendous impact on me and contributed to my success. He has never shied away from a challenge because he has always had the courage to try.

> The crowd was yelling as tears were running in my mouth. The white line was clearly visible, as I started to feel the end of the race was in sight. With my arm dangling at my side, I slowly moved across the finish line. I had finished the race!

> I accomplished what I had started and my journey was complete. I was so relieved to have it behind me and at the same time so proud of my accomplishment. Each hurdle was a struggle, but through perseverance and determination I was made whole.

Dorothy (me) was able to return to her family, only to discover she was with them the entire time. I have been striving for a dream that in reality, I had already achieved.

The graduation ceremony was finally here and my internal debate to walk across the stage was constantly weighing on my mind. Deep down in my soul, I really wanted to place the robe and hat on my body and be handed the personalized diploma. Doug urged me to go through the traditional process and was particularly excited about the prospect of Bailey and me walking across the stage one after the other on graduation day, but due to the fact that we didn't graduate in the same semester the school would not allow it. I really wanted to don the cap and gown and be handed the personalized diploma. However, I knew that six months our family would be celebrating Bailey's graduation and twice in six months was too much to ask of everyone.

It was the night before the commencement ceremony when suddenly it hit me I didn't want to leave town for Christmas with my family without my diploma in hand. I wanted to show my parents that their hard work regarding my education had finally paid off. Their daughter had finally earned her degree.

Realizing I had missed the opportunity to possess my diploma before the holidays, I sent an e-mail late in the evening to the staff member in charge of the graduation event. She returned my call early the next morning. "You have changed your mind about walking in the procession," she immediately said. "No," I replied, "I just want my diploma to show my parents for Christmas." Without hesitation she informed she was headed to a local pancake house near the university and could bring a certain certificate with her to the humble establishment. I jumped to my feet, woke up Doug, threw on my sweat pants and grabbed my colored Santa hat that I had received at the recent office party. I couldn't wait for my slow moving husband, as I informed him I would grab a table for an impromptu celebration breakfast.

I started down the University Drive in my ridiculous Santa hat on my head, feeling the deepest thrill of excitement. I was going to receive my college degree! My journey of seven years of hard work and sacrifice was coming to a close combined with the many "hurdles" along the way. My yellow road had come to an end and one of my most cherished goals was accomplished.

As I entered the crowded restaurant I spotted the university staff member standing up in the back of the room waving for my attention. In her hands contained my coveted college diploma, along with a big smile over the uniqueness of our private ceremony. I ran straight up to her she extended her arm to hand me the diploma, but I did not reach for it until I excitedly asked her to flip the silly snowball on the end of the colored hat. As she reached for the furry tassel and moved it from one side of my head to the other, I felt a rush of pride and accomplishment. The movement of the tassel represented the culmination of many details in my life over the last five years. The joy combined with sadness including raising three children, battling cancer, the deaths of a sister, death of a mother-in-law, death of a brother, five surgeries, two adult bullies, working full time, moving three times, starting a business while journaling it all to maintain my emotional sanity.

As the tassel passed across my face and what appeared to be a split of a second felt like a lifetime of determination. As she placed the diploma in my hand I was overcome with emotion and I burst into tears. The nearby diners sensed our private ceremony and responded with spontaneous clap of approval. As if on cue, Doug entered the restaurant minutes later and found his wife weeping uncontrollably. With a look of confusion on his face Doug calmly asked me if I was going to be ok as the tears dripped hysterically down my face.

Tears

tears of joy, tears of pain
tears of my loved ones caring for me through all the insane
tears of hopelessness, tears of fear
tears of sadness which have been in my life for several years
tears of laughter, tears of love
my tears are ever flowing like the soaring of a dove

December 19, 2008

The degree was a mere piece of paper but in reality it signified so much more. Graduating from college at my age was a direct result of determination made possible by the love and support of my family and friends who never allowed me to give up. Throughout this experience I came to the realization that it is our responsibility and to others to be thankful for each day, to live each day as if it were our last and to encourage others to embrace their dream with a loving heart.

All of my struggles became blessings and my disease gave me an inner strength and confidence to pursue my dreams. These hurdles graced me with a new passion to **embrace** this time in my life with gratitude and thankfulness regardless of how good or bad the current situation is and always keep in mind it is vital to surround yourself with people who can lift you up. Always be open and **experience** life with a loving and forgiving heart and take on the responsibility to **encourage** those around you with genuine respect and compassion. The three *E's* have served me well.

Through this entire experience I have learned to open my heart and mind. Everyone has hurdles in their life and there is no more important a hurdle than the one right in front of you. Taking "Baby Steps" and living "One Day at a Time" enables us to endure and survive.

"Lessons Learned"

Life gets that much harder,
It makes you that much stronger,
Oh, some pages turned,
Some bridges burned,
But there were,
Lessons learned.

Written by Diane Warren, Recorded by Carrie Underwood

About the Author

When asked to write the *About the Author* for my mother's book I was initially disinterested. How can one sit down and brainstorm thoughts that describe and inform an audience about your own mother.

I procrastinated the assignment until the last possible second and basically had to force myself to sit down and describe my mother to a bunch of people who do not know her and will probably never meet her.

Nancy Woodson is an individual who takes pride in her family. Ever since I was a small child, I was uncomfortable with my mother constantly doting on my sisters and me. She takes pride in her children and has helped me become the person that I am today. As I grew older I realized that she did not do it to make me feel awkward she did it because she loved me, and the things that I had accomplished. She cares for those around her and makes it a personal goal to help the important people in her life as much as she can. Even though these are all wonderful attributes (and hopefully you can realize that you are about to read about a great woman/ mother/ wife/ child/ sister/friend/ mentor/role model), attributes alone are not enough to draw a reader to a book.

Nancy Woodson is a person who has undergone a complete transformation, from childhood in Memphis Tennessee to socialite country club life in Fort Worth Texas. She attended four Universities in the past two decades that might be a record for a person to obtain an undergraduate degree in general studies. She began the first 15 years of her marriage as a homemaker and now she has worked for multiple employers, started a small business and written an autobiography about her life. All of this was accomplished while raising a family and wrestling with cancer.

It is hard to recognize how arduous a person's journey has been when it develops right under your nose. She has overcome cancer, dysfunctional relatives, educational restraints and never-ending battles with her children. Her life story has been marked by tragedies, miracles, disappointments, satisfaction, despair and happiness. If there is one thing that I have learned as the son of Nancy Woodson, "just take it one day at a time." Life is a rollercoaster, with ups and downs and twists and turns. Without the bad there is no way to enjoy the good and that kind of philosophy is the reason Nancy Woodson has found eternal happiness with her family and friends.

I am not here to tell you that my mother is the most wonderful woman in the world. Quite honestly, she is more than a handful and at times very unreasonable. I am here to tell you that she is a human, no super powers, no epic adventures and she is more easily defeated by injustice than kryptonite. Her story is unique, her journey unpredictable and her love for her passions, immeasurable.

By Jay Woodson
Age 21

My husband Doug stood by me and
shouldered the added responsibility
of caring for our three children while
working full-time, diagnosed with
thyroid cancer and returned to college
to complete my undergraduate degree.
On nights when I had to prepare for
a test, he would serve me dinner on a
tray, draw my bath and pull back my bed. Doug's encouragement and true
love gave me super-human strength. I often questioned my overloaded
schedule resulting in extreme exhaustion and total frustration, but
he would settle me down with his calm spirit. It was Doug who was
instrumental in accomplishing my dream of becoming an author as he
became the third and final editor of this memoir Hurdles.

As with many couples our marriage has had its bumps, but "Our
struggles have become our biggest blessings." This unselfish man has
given me the best part of himself as well as his unconditional love and
guidance. For this I am forever grateful. I have grown and matured into
a more productive and confident woman and I applaud my husband for
putting aside any ego and simply encouraging his wife.

Breinigsville, PA USA
01 February 2011
254622BV00001B/50/P